Lonely Planet

Pocket
AMSTERDAM
TOP SIGHTS · LOCAL LIFE · MADE EASY

D0039804

Karla Zimmerman

In This Book

QuickStart Guide

Your keys to understanding the city – we help you decide what to do and how to do it

Need to Know
Tips for a smooth trip

Neighbourhoods
What's where

Explore Amsterdam

The best things to see and do, neighbourhood by neighbourhood

Top Sights
Make the most of your visit

Local Life
The insider's city

The Best of Amsterdam

The city's highlights in handy lists to help you plan

Best Walks
See the city on foot

Amsterdam's Best...
The best experiences

Survival Guide

Tips and tricks for a seamless, hassle-free city experience

Getting Around
Travel like a local

Essential Information
Including where to stay

Our selection of the city's best places to eat, drink and experience:

⦿ **Sights**

✖ **Eating**

🍷 **Drinking**

✪ **Entertainment**

🔒 **Shopping**

. . . .

These symbols give you the vital information for each listing:

☏ Telephone Numbers	👪 Family-Friendly
⊘ Opening Hours	🐾 Pet-Friendly
P Parking	🚌 Bus
⊖ Nonsmoking	🛳 Ferry
@ Internet Access	Ⓜ Metro
🛜 Wi-Fi Access	🚊 Tram
🥗 Vegetarian Selection	🚆 Train
📖 English-Language Menu	

. . . .

Find each listing quickly on maps for each neighbourhood:

Bar Hemingway

16 🍷 Map p233, B2

Legend has it that Hemi self, wielding a machine erate this timber-pan tered bar during shawpiaaa in a en by Papa ar s.com; Hôtel Rit ⊘6.30pm-2a

6 ⦿ Plac Vo

Lonely Planet's Amsterdam

Lonely Planet Pocket Guides are designed to get you straight to the heart of the city.

Inside you'll find all the must-see sights, plus tips to make your visit to each one really memorable. We've split the city into easy-to-navigate neighbourhoods and provided clear maps so you'll find your way around with ease. Our expert authors have searched out the best of the city: walks, food, nightlife and shopping, to name a few. Because you want to explore, our 'Local Life' pages will take you to some of the most exciting areas to experience the real Amsterdam.

And of course you'll find all the practical tips you need for a smooth trip: itineraries for short visits, how to get around, and how much to tip the guy who serves you a drink at the end of a long day's exploration.

It's your guarantee of a really great experience.

Our Promise

You can trust our travel information because Lonely Planet authors visit the places we write about, each and every edition. We never accept freebies for positive coverage, so you can rely on us to tell it like it is.

QuickStart Guide 7

Explore Amsterdam 21

Worth a Trip:

The Best of Amsterdam 149

Amsterdam's Best Walks

Amsterdam's Best ...

Survival Guide 171

QuickStart Guide

Welcome to Amsterdam

Amsterdam works its fairy-tale magic in many ways: via the gabled, Golden Age buildings; glinting, boat-filled canals; and especially the cosy, centuries-old brown cafes, where candles burn low and beers froth high. Add in mega art museums and funky street markets, and it's easy to see why this atmospheric city is one of Europe's most popular getaways.

One of Amsterdam's picturesque canals
EYE35.PIX / ALAMY ©

Amsterdam
Top Sights

Van Gogh Museum (p86)

You'll wait in line outside and jostle with the crowds inside, but seeing those vivid brushstrokes of yellow sunflowers and purple-blue irises makes it all worthwhile.

INGOLF POMPE / GETTY IMAGES©

MARK R THOMAS / GETTY IMAGES ©

Vondelpark (p92)

On sunny days it seems the whole city converges on this sprawling urban idyll. Joggers, picnickers, kissing couples, accordion players and frolicking children all throng the lawns, thickets and cafes.

Rijksmuseum (p90)

The Netherlands' top treasure house bursts with Golden Age paintings, blue-and-white Delft pottery and gilded dollhouses. Rembrandt's humungous, gape-worthy *Night Watch* leads the pack.

TONY BURNS / GETTY IMAGES ©

PHOTOS 12 / ALAMY ©

Anne Frank Huis (p44)

Walking through the Secret Annexe, standing in Anne's melancholy bedroom and seeing the red-plaid diary itself is an undeniably powerful experience that draws a million visitors annually.

Royal Palace (Koninklijk Paleis) (p24)

Enter the Queen's digs and ogle the tapestries, chandeliers, Italian marble and frescoed ceilings while getting a history lesson in Dutch royalty and politics.

Museum het Rembrandthuis (p124)

Step into the Dutch icon's inner sanctum and immerse yourself in his studio, where soft light streams in through the windows and seashells, animal horns and other exotica weigh down the shelves.

Amsterdam Local Life

Insider tips to help you find the real city

After doing the tourist sights, seek out the offbeat music clubs, bohemian artist quarters, sweet patisseries and quirky local shops that make up the locals' Amsterdam. Count on brown cafes and canals making appearances.

Shopping the Jordaan & Western Canals (p46)

▶ Small, oddball shops
▶ Cafes
▶ Vintage & farmers markets

You probably didn't realise you needed antique eyeglasses, artisanal cheese or a hand-bound art book. But these surprises happen as you ramble through the enchanted web of Jordaan lanes. The other thing that happens: you'll get lost. No worries. Atmospheric cafes pop up to lend a guiding beverage.

Discovering Bohemian De Pijp (p104)

▶ Ethnic eateries
▶ Amsterdam's biggest market
▶ Music venues

De Pijp is like its own little village: people from many walks of life – workers, intellectuals, immigrants, prostitutes – mingle at the neighbourhood-spanning street market, then take the conversation to the jazzy little corner cafes and cool-cat clubs.

Strolling the Southern Canal Belt (p68)

▶ Golden Age mansions
▶ Swanky antique shops
▶ Flower market

Get a feel for posh Amsterdam around the Southern Canals, one of the city's most exclusive addresses from the get-go. Seventeenth-century millionaires built doublewide homes here, and today's classy touches include the colourful flower market, the antique quarter and opulent theatres.

Cafe-Hopping in Nieuwmarkt & Plantage (p126)

▶ Flea market
▶ Cafes in historic buildings
▶ Arts centre

Among the city's oldest, leafiest districts, Nieuwmarkt and the Plantage have an embarrassment of riches when it comes to places to relax and swill. No wonder locals flock here to hang out in between browsing through markets and gazing at contemporary art.

Cafe life, Nieuwmarkt (p126)

Exploring Westerpark & Western Islands (p64)

▶ Amsterdam School architecture
▶ Edgy cultural park
▶ Foodie-favourite fare

Amsterdam doesn't get much cooler than these two enclaves in the city's northwest corner. Get ready for drawbridge-strewn islands and a sprawling green space that melds bird-rich marshes with DJ-spinning cafes and theatres.

Cyclists, De Pijp (p104)

Other great places to experience the city like a local:

De Twee Zwaantjes (p57)

Wil Graanstra Friteshuis (p56)

Tokoman (p134)

Villa Zeezicht (p34)

Reguliersgracht (p74)

Kingfisher (p112)

Oudemanhuis Book Market (p28)

Café Toussaint (p98)

Utrechtsestraat (p83)

Oosterpark (p120)

Amsterdam
Day Planner

Day One

Begin with the biggies: tram to the Museum Quarter to ogle the masterpieces at the **Van Gogh Museum** (p86) and **Rijksmuseum** (p90). They'll be crowded, so make sure you've prebooked tickets. Modern art buffs might want to swap in the **Stedelijk Museum** (p95) for one of the others. They're all lined up in a walkable row.

Spend the afternoon in the medieval City Centre. Have lunch at slow-food favourite **Gartine** (p30). Explore the secret courtyard and gardens at the **Begijnhof** (p28). Walk up the street to the **Dam** (p28), where the **Royal Palace** (p24), **Nicuwe Kerk** (p29) and Nationaal Monument huddle and provide a dose of Dutch history. Bend over and take your *jenever* (Dutch gin) like a local at **Wynand Fockink** (p34).

Do elegant Dutch for dinner at **Hemelse Modder** (p133). Then venture into the Red Light District. A walk down Warmoesstraat or Oudezijds Achterburgwal provides an eye-popping line-up of fetish gear shops, live sex shows, smoky coffeeshops and, of course, women in day-glo lingerie beckoning from crimson windows. Then settle in to a brown cafe, such as **Café In 't Aepjen** (p34), **In de Olofspoort** (p35) or **'t Mandje** (p35).

Day Two

Browse the **Albert Cuypmarkt** (p104), Amsterdam's largest street bazaar, an international free-for-all of cheeses, fish, *stroopwafels* (syrup waffles) and bargain-priced clothing. Then submit to the **Heineken Experience** (p107) to get shaken up, heated up and 'bottled' like the beer you'll drink at the end of the brewery tour.

Have lunch at **Bazar Amsterdam** (p109) or one of the other ethnic eateries lining Albert Cuypstraat. Make your way over to the Southern Canal Belt and stroll along the grand **Golden Bend** (p69). Visit **Museum Van Loon** (p72) for a peek into the opulent canal-house lifestyle, or see the lifestyle with a dose of kitty quirk at the **Kattenkabinet** (p69) Tour the glinting waterways with **Boom Chicago Boats** (p157) or **Blue Boat Company** (p157).

Splash out at Indonesian **Blue Pepper** (p96) for dinner. Then it's time to par-tee at hyperactive, neon-lit Leidseplein. If you get here before 7.30pm weekdays (6pm weekends), check at the **Uitburo** (p80) for concerts or show tickets. **Paradiso** (p79) and **Melkweg** (p79) host the coolest agendas. Otherwise the good-time clubs and cafes around the square beckon. Try beery **Café de Spuyt** (p77) or historic **Eijlders** (p76).

Short on time?
We've arranged Amsterdam's must-sees into these day-by-day itineraries to make sure you see the very best of the city in the time you have available.

Day Three

☼ Explore the Harbour and Eastern Docklands' cutting-edge design. Stop in at **ARCAM** (p142) to arm yourself with architectural information, then head onward to the sea treasures at **het Scheepvaartmuseum** (p142) and views from **NEMO** (p143) and the **Centrale Bibliotheek Amsterdam** (p143).

☼ Go west – as in Western Canals – and fork into sweet or savoury traditional Dutch **Pancakes!** (p53). Immerse yourself in the surrounding **Negen Straatjes** (p47) (Nine Streets), a tic-tac-toe board of oddball speciality shops. The **Anne Frank Huis** (p44) is also in the neighbourhood, and it's a must. The claustrophobic rooms, their windows still covered with blackout screens, give an all-too-real feel for Anne's life in hiding.

☾ Spend the evening in the Jordaan, the chummy district touted as the Amsterdam of yore. Tables of tapas spill out into the street from **La Oliva** (p54). Kitschy **Moeders** (p54) cooks up traditional Dutch dishes. Afterwards, hoist a glass on a canalside terrace at **Café 't Smalle** (p56), join the drunken sing-along at **De Twee Zwaantjes** (p57), or quaff beers at heaps of other *gezellig* haunts.

Day Four

☼ Take a spin through **Waterlooplein Flea Market** (p127). Doc Martens? Buddha statues? Electric saw? These goods and more fill the stalls. Rembrandt sure loved markets, if his nearby studio is any indication. **Museum het Rembrandthuis** (p124) gives a peek at the master's inner sanctum, including his curio-packed cabinet and paint-spattered easel. Neighbouring **Gassan Diamonds** (p132) gives the bling lowdown via free tours.

☼ Mosey over to the Plantage for a pizza and prosecco at **De Pizzabakkers** (p133). Hopefully you won't lose your lunch when viewing the early inking implements at the **Amsterdam Tattoo Museum** (p130). Next it's time for an only-in-Amsterdam experience: drinking organic beer at the foot of an authentic windmill at **Brouwerij 't IJ** (p134). Snap your photos before knocking back too many glasses of the strong suds.

☾ You've been a sightseeing trooper, zipping through most of Amsterdam's neighbourhoods over the past four days. An evening spent plopped on **De Ysbreeker** (p120)'s terrace, looking out over the bustling, houseboat-strewn Amstel river, is a well-deserved treat.

Need to Know

For more information, see Survival Guide (p172)

Currency
Euro (€)

Language
Dutch and English

Visas
Generally not required for stays up to three months. Some nationalities require a Schengen visa.

Money
ATMs widely available. Credit cards accepted in most hotels but not all restaurants. Non-European credit cards are sometimes rejected.

Mobile Phones
Local SIM cards can be used in European and Australian phones. Standard North American GSM 1900 phones will not work.

Time
Central European Time (GMT/UTC plus one hour).

Plugs & Adaptors
Plugs have two round pins; electrical current is 220V. North American visitors will require an adaptor and a transformer.

Tipping
Tip 5% to 10% in restaurants and taxis, or just round up to the next euro. Give hotel porters a few euros.

① Before You Go

Your Daily Budget

Budget less than €100
► Dorm bed €22–€35
► Supermarkets and lunchtime specials for food €15
► Boom Chicago discount ticket €17

Midrange €100–€200
► Double room €125
► Three-course dinner in casual restaurant €30
► Concertgebouw ticket €40

Top end more than €200
► Four-star hotel double room €230
► Five-course dinner in top restaurant €50
► Private canal boat rental for two hours €90

Useful Websites

► **Lonely Planet** (www.lonelyplanet.com/amsterdam) Destination information, hotel bookings, traveller forum and more.

► **I Amsterdam** (www.iamsterdam.com) City-run portal packed with sightseeing, accommodation and event info.

► **Time Out Amsterdam** (www.timeout.com/amsterdam) Cultural features and listings.

Advance Planning

► **Six months** Book your hotel, especially if you'll be visiting in summer.

► **Two months** Check calendars for the Concertgebouw, Muziekgebouw aan 't IJ, Melkweg and Paradiso, and buy tickets.

► **One week** Buy tickets online to the Van Gogh Museum, Anne Frank Huis and Rijksmuseum. Book walking and cycling tours and make reservations at top restaurants.

② Arriving in Amsterdam

Most people flying to Amsterdam arrive at Schiphol International Airport (AMS; www .schiphol.nl), 18km southwest of the city centre. National and international trains arrive at Centraal Station (CS) in the city centre.

✈ From Schiphol Airport

Destination	Best Transport
City Centre/Jordaan	Train to Centraal Station
Nieuwmarkt/Plantage	Train to Centraal Station
De Pijp/Southern Canal Belt (except Leidseplein)	Train to Centraal Station
Old South/Vondelpark/ Leidseplein	Bus 197

🚊 From Centraal Station

Destination	Best Transport
City Centre & Red Light District	Tram 4, 9, 16, 24, 25
Jordaan & Western Canals	Tram 1, 2, 5, 13
Southern Canal Belt	Tram 1, 2, 5 for Leidseplein; Tram 4, 9 for Rembrandtplein
Old South & Vondelpark	Tram 1, 2, 5
De Pijp	Tram 16, 24
Nieuwmarkt & Plantago	Tram 9

At the Airport/Train Station

Schiphol Airport ATMs, currency exchanges, tourist info, car hire, train tickets, luggage storage, shopping mall and food court.

Centraal Station ATMs, currency exchanges, tourist info, restaurants, shops, luggage storage and train tickets.

③ Getting Around

Walking and cycling are the primary ways to travel around the small, densely packed city. GVB passes in chip-card form are the most convenient option for public transport. Buy them at VVV offices or from tram conductors. Always wave your card at the pink-logoed machine when entering and departing.

Walking

Central Amsterdam is compact and easy to cover by foot.

🚲 Bicycle

Cycling is locals' main mode of getting around. Rental companies are all over town; bikes cost about €12.50 per day.

🚊 Tram

Trams are fast, frequent and ubiquitous, operating between 6am and 12.30am. A one-hour fare is €2.70, a day-pass is €7.50.

🚌 Bus

The bus system primarily serves the outer districts; it's not much use in the city centre. Same fare as trams.

Ⓜ Metro

Similarly to the bus system, the metro system mainly serves the outer district.

⛴ Ferry

Free ferries depart for northern Amsterdam from docks behind Centraal Station.

🚕 Taxi

Taxis are expensive and not very speedy given Amsterdam's maze of streets. Fares are €1.95 per km; the meter starts at €2.65.

Amsterdam
Neighbourhoods

City Centre (p22)
The busiest section of town for visitors, Amsterdam's medieval core mixes fairy-tale Golden Age buildings, brown cafes and the lurid Red Light District.

◉ Top Sights

Royal Palace (Koninklijk Paleis)

Jordaan & Western Canals (p42)
The Jordaan teems with cosy pubs and lanes ideal for getting lost. The Western Canals unfurl quirky boutiques and waterside cafes.

◉ Top Sights

Anne Frank Huis

Vondelpark & Old South (p84)
Vondelpark is a green lung with personality, adjacent to the genteel Old South, home to Amsterdam's grandest museums.

◉ Top Sights

Van Gogh Museum

Rijksmuseum

Vondelpark

De Pijp (p102)
Ethnic meets trendy in this recently gentrified neighbourhood, best sampled at the colourful Albert Cuypmarkt and the multicultural eateries that surround it.

Anne Frank Huis

Royal Palace (Koninklijk Paleis)

Vondelpark
Rijksmuseum
Van Gogh Museum

Harbour & Eastern Docklands (p138)
The harbour's hip, ever-changing skyline extends into the edge Eastern Docklands, adored by the design clique for its architectural experimentation.

Nieuwmarkt & Plantage (p122)
See Rembrandt's studio and Amsterdam's Jewish heritage in Nieuwmarkt, and gardens and a beery windmill in the Plantage.

👁 **Top Sights**
Museum het Rembrandthuis

👁 *Museum het Rembrandthuis*

Southern Canal Belt (p00)
By day, visit the city's less-heralded museums. By night, party at the clubs around Leidseplein and Rembrandtplein.

Oosterpark & Around (p114)
The Oost is one of the city's most culturally diverse neighbourhoods, with Moroccan and Turkish enclaves and some great trendsetting clubs.

Explore
Amsterdam

Worth a Trip

Damrak, near Centraal Station, City Centre
MARTIN BOND / ALAMY ©

Explore

City Centre

Amsterdam's heart beats in its medieval core. The Royal Palace rises up on the main square, but the main thing to do is wander the twisting lanes past 17th-century pubs, hidden gardens and wee speciality shops. As for the infamous Red Light District, far from being a no-go area, it has some beautiful historic cafes, plus the stunning Oude Kerk.

The Sights in a Day

☼ Fuel up with coffee and pastries at **Lanskroon** (p33). Nearby, look for the secret courtyard at the **Begijnhof** (p28). Pop into the **Amsterdam Museum** (p28) to learn local history, then see it in person at the **Dam** (p28), where the city was founded. The 15th-century **Nieuwe Kerk** (p29) and 17th-century **Royal Palace** (p24) also huddle here.

☼ Grab a sandwich at **'Skek** (p33), and prepare to venture into the Red Light District. There's more here than you think. The 700-year-old **Oude Kerk** (p29) has a who's who of famous folks buried beneath its floor, while **Museum Ons' Lieve Heer op Solder** (p30) hides an entire, relic-rich church behind its canal-house facade. You can see titillating stuff too: walk down Warmoesstraat or Oudezijds Achterburgwal, past **Absolute Danny** (p40) and **Casa Rosso** (p37).

☾ Fork into *stamppot* and other Dutch specialities at **Haesje Claes** (p33). To try the famed Dutch *jenever* (gin), belly up to the bar at **Wynand Fockink** (p34) or **In de Olofspoort** (p35). Or sip at **Hoppe** (p34) on the Spui, a cafe-ringed plaza that is the city's intellectual hub.

◉ Top Sights
Royal Palace (p24)

♥ Best of Amsterdam

Eating
Gartine (p30)

'Skek (p33)

Lanskroon (p33)

Drinking
Wynand Fockink (p34)

Hoppe (p34)

Café In 't Aepjen (p34)

Museums & Galleries
Amsterdam Museum (p28)

Museum Ons' Lieve Heer op Solder (p30)

Shopping
Condomerie Het Gulden Vlies (p39)

Absolute Danny (p40)

Getting There

🚊 **Tram** Numerous tram lines go through the neighbourhood en route to Centraal Station (most via the Dam) including trams 1, 2, 4, 6, 9, 13, 16, 17, 24, 25 and 26.

⚓ **Boat** Free ferries run to Amsterdam-Noord, departing from the piers behind Centraal Station.

Top Sights
Royal Palace (Koninklijk Paleis)

Welcome to the Queen's house. If she's away, you're welcome to come in and wander around. Today's Royal Palace began life as a glorified town hall, and was completed in 1665. The architect, Jacob van Campen, spared no expense to display Amsterdam's wealth in a way that rivalled the grandest European buildings of the day. The result is opulence on a grand scale.

 Map p26, B5

☎620 40 60

www.paleisamsterdam.nl

The Dam

adult/child €7.50/3.75

⊙11am-5pm daily Jul & Aug, noon-5pm Tue-Sun Sep-Jun

The great *burgerzaal* (citizens' hall)

Don't Miss

The Tribunal
Start at the ground floor's Tribunal. This was the original court where magistrates meted out death sentences. The sinister sculptures of skulls and serpents underscore the chamber's severe purpose.

The Halls' Treasures
Most of the palace's rooms spread over the 1st floor, which is awash in chandeliers (51 shiners in total), damasks, gilded clocks and rich paintings by Ferdinand Bol and Jacob de Wit. The great *burgerzaal* (citizens' hall) that occupies the heart of the building was envisioned as a schematic of the world, with Amsterdam as its centre. Check out the maps inlaid in the floor; they show the eastern and western hemispheres, with a 1654 celestial map plopped in the middle. The archways hold sculptures representing the four elements: birds (air), fish (water), fruit (earth) and fire.

King Louis' Gifts
In 1808 the building became the palace of King Louis, Napoleon Bonaparte's brother. In a classic slip-up in the new lingo, French-born Louis told his subjects here that he was the 'rabbit *(konijn)* of Holland', whereas he meant 'king' *(konink)*. Napoleon dismissed him two years later. Louis left behind about 1000 pieces of Empire-style furniture and decorative artworks. As a result, the palace now holds one of the world's largest collections from the period.

Today's Palace
Officially Queen Beatrix lives here and pays a symbolic rent, though she really shacks up in Den Haag. The palace is still used to entertain foreign heads of state and for other official business.

☑ Top Tips

▶ Pick up a free audio tour at the desk after you enter. It's available in Dutch, English, German, French, Italian and Spanish, and greatly enhances a visit, since there isn't much signage to explain what you're seeing.

▶ The palace often closes for state functions, especially during April, May, November and December. The website posts the schedule; check before heading over.

▶ The palace does not accept advance reservations, nor any type of discount card, so all visitors must line up at the main entrance. Queues typically are shorter late in the afternoon.

✕ Take a Break

Sample the famed Dutch herring on a fluffy white roll at Rob Wigboldus Vishandel (p32). Wash it down with the strong brews at Café Belgique (p35).

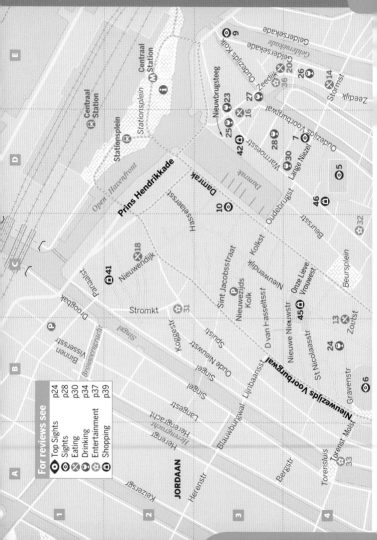

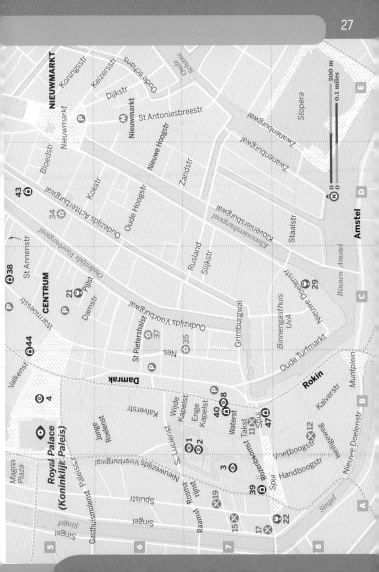

NIEUWMARKT

Koningsstr
Keizersstr
Oude schans
Oude Schans
Dijkstr
Nieuwmarkt
Nieuwmarkt
St Antoniesbreestr

Bloedstr
Koestr
Nieuwe Hoogstr
Zandstr
Stopera

43
34
Oudezijds Achterburgwal
Oude Hoogstr
Zwanenburgwal
Zwanenburgwal
Zwanenburgwal

38
St Annenstr
Oudezijds Voorburgwal
Rusland
Kloveniersburgwal
Slijkstr
Staalstr
Amstel

CENTRUM
21
Prijlst
Damstr
Warmoesstr
Binnen Amstel

44
St Pietershalst
Oudezijds Voorburgwal
Nes
Grimburgwal
Binnengasthuis UvA
Nieuwe Doelenstr
29

37
35
Oude Turfmarkt

Damrak
Rokin
Muntplein

4
Wijde Kapelstr
Enge Kapelst
40
8
Waterst
Kalverstr
Nieuwe Doelenstr

Kalverstr
11
Sp
47
12
Rokin
Heiligeweg

Royal Palace
(Koninklijk Paleis)
Jonge Roelenst
S Luciensteeg
Nieuwezijds Voorburgwal
1
2
Rokinomst Takst
Voetboogstr

Magna Plaza
Gasthuismolenst Paleisstr
Rosma rijnst
3
Handboogstr

Singel
Spuistr
19
39
Spui
22

Singel
Singel
Raamsteeg
15
17
Singel

200 m
0.1 miles
N
Amstel

Sights

Amsterdam Museum
MUSEUM

1 ⊙ Map p26, B7

The city's history museum keeps getting spiffier, thanks to ongoing renovations. Start with the multimedia DNA exhibit, which breaks down Amsterdam's 1000-year history into seven whiz-bang time periods. Afterward, plunge into the lower floors to see troves of religious artifacts, porcelain and paintings. Extra points for finding Rembrandt's macabre *Anatomy Lesson of Dr Deijman*. Bring your smartphone to scan exhibit barcodes for extra features. (☏523 18 22; www.amsterdam museum.nl; Kalverstraat 92; adult/child €10/5; ⊙10am-5pm; 🚊1/2/5 Spui)

Local Life

Oudemanhuis Book Market

To rub tweed-patched elbows with professors browsing 19th-century copies of *Das Kapital* and Icelandic sagas, head to the **Oudemanhuis Book Market** (Oude-manhuispoort; ⊙11am-4pm Mon-Fri; 🚊4/9/14/16/24/25 Spui). The venerable little bazaar hides in a moody old covered alleyway between Oudezijds Achterburgwal and Kloveniersburgwal by the University of Amsterdam. Most of the secondhand tomes are in Dutch, though a few English-language classics turn up, too.

Civic Guard Gallery
GALLERY

2 ⊙ Map p26, B7

This cool gallery is part of the Amsterdam Museum, and fills an alleyway next to the entrance. It displays grand posed group portraits, from medieval guards painted during the Dutch Golden Age (à la Rembrandt's *Night Watch*) to *Modern Civic Guards*, a rendering of Anne Frank, Alfred Heineken and a joint-smoking personification of Amsterdam. (Kalverstraat 92; admission free; ⊙10am-5pm; 🚊1/2/5 Spui)

Begijnhof
HISTORIC BUILDINGS

3 ⊙ Map p26, A7

This veiled courtyard of tiny houses and gardens was built in the 14th century for the Beguines, a lay Catholic sisterhood. Two churches hide here: a 'clandestine' chapel (1671), where the Beguines worshipped in secret from the Calvinists; and the English Church (c 1392), where Puritans congregated. Both are usually open for browsing. The wooden house at No 34 (c 1465) is the Netherlands' oldest. (☏622 19 18; www.begijnhofamsterdam.nl; main entrance off Gedempte Begijnensloot; admission free; ⊙8am-5pm; 🚊1/2/5 Spui)

Dam
SQUARE

4 ⊙ Map p26, B5

The southern part of the square was the divine spot where Amsterdam was founded in around 1270. Now it's a local hangout filled with buskers; carnival rides add to the fun in springtime. The obelisk on the east side is the

Begijnhof

Nationaal Monument, built in 1956 to honour WWII's fallen. The 12 urns at the rear hold earth from war cemeteries of the 11 provinces and the Dutch East Indies. (🚊4/9/16/24/25 Dam)

Oude Kerk CHURCH

5 ◎ Map p26, D4

It's an intriguing contradiction: Red Light windows surround the 14th-century church (which is Amsterdam's oldest building). Inside, check out the Müller organ, naughty choir stall carvings and famous Amsterdammers' tombstones in the floor (such as Rembrandt's wife Saskia). The church holds Sunday services at 11am, but generally it hosts exhibitions such as the World Press Photo Show. You can

also climb the tower. (Old Church; ☏625 82 84; www.oudekerk.nl; Oudekerksplein 23; adult/child €8/6; ⏰11am-5pm Mon-Sat, 1-5pm Sun; 🚊4/9/16/24/25 Dam)

Nieuwe Kerk CHURCH

6 ◎ Map p26, B4

Nieuwe Kerk (dating from 1408 – it's all relative) is the historic stage of Dutch coronations and royal weddings. Other than such ceremonies, the building no longer functions as a church, but rather a hall for art and cultural exhibitions. For a free peek, slip through the gift shop (by the entrance) and upstairs for a display on the church's history. (New Church; ☏638 69 09; www.nieuwekerk.nl;

The Dam; adult/child €8/free; ⏰10am-5pm; 🚊1/2/5/13/14/17 Raadhuisstraat)

Museum Ons' Lieve Heer op Solder

MUSEUM

7 ⊚ Map p26, D4

What looks like an ordinary canal house turns out to have an entire Catholic church stashed inside. Ons' Lieve Heer op Solder (Our Dear Lord in the Attic) was built in the mid-1600s in defiance of the Calvinists. Inside you'll see labyrinthine staircases, rich artworks, period decor and the soaring, two-storey church itself. The museum is undergoing restoration through 2013, so some artefacts have been put away temporarily. (✆624 66 04; www.opsolder.nl; Oudezijds Voorburgwal 40; adult/child €8/4; ⏰10am-5pm Mon-Sat, 1-5pm Sun; 🚊4/9/16/24/25 Centraal Station)

Noord/Zuidlijn Viewpoint

LOOKOUT

8 ⊚ Map p26, B7

Descend the stairs across from Rokin 96 and behold the north–south metro line excavation in action. The massive engineering project is like a sci-fi movie: an abyss filled with muck and pipes and colossal digging machines. The whole place rumbles when a tram passes overhead. The displays and signage are in Dutch, but English-speaking guides often are on hand. (www.noordzuidlijn.amsterdam.nl; across from Rokin 96; ⏰1-6pm Tue-Sun; 🚊4/9/14/16/24/25 Rokin)

Schreierstoren

HISTORIC BUILDING

9 ⊚ Map p26, E3

Built around 1480 as part of the city's defenses, Henry Hudson set sail for the New World from this tower in 1609; a plaque outside marks the spot. It's called the 'wailing tower' in lore – where women waved farewell to sailors' ships – but the name actually comes from the word 'sharp' (for how the corner jutted into the bay). Step into the VOC Cafe for a look inside the structure. (www.schreierstoren.nl; Prins Hendrikkade 94-95; 🚊4/9/16/24/25 Centraal Station)

Sexmuseum Amsterdam

MUSEUM

10 ⊚ Map p26, D3

The Sexmuseum is good for a giggle. You'll find replicas of pornographic Pompeian plates, erotic 14th-century Viennese bronzes, some of the world's earliest nude photographs, an automated farting flasher in a trench coat and a music box that plays 'Edelweiss' and purports to show a couple in flagrante delicto. (www.sexmuseumamsterdam.nl; Damrak 18; admission €4, 16yr & over only; ⏰9.30am-11.30pm; 🚊4/9/16/24/25 Centraal Station)

Eating

Gartine

CAFE €€

11 ✕ Map p26, B7

Gartine serves delectable breakfast pastries, sandwiches and salads from

Understand

Red Light District & Legalised Prostitution

As much as the tourism board wishes it weren't so, the Red Light District – aka De Wallen (The Quays) – is a distinguishing feature of Amsterdam. Perhaps what's most fascinating is that it's not a festering den of sleaze. Granted, lads on lost weekends don't set a great tone, but this may be the safest vice zone in the world.

No Big Deal

To the Dutch, legal prostitution is simply an industry like any other. Still, it's mind-bending when you first set eyes on the women in the windows, illuminated not only with red lights (because it's the most flattering hue), but also with black ones that make their white lingerie glow enticingly. Your first instinct might be to take a photo, but don't do it – out of simple respect, and to avoid having your camera tossed in a canal by the ladies' enforcers.

You'll see specialisation – an NL sticker in a window, indicating 'Dutch spoken here', and sections occupied by women from Suriname, Russia or Latin America – and of course aggressive self-marketing. Women pay to rent a window for an eight- or 10-hour shift; they also pay income taxes based on city estimates of income correlated with tourism figures. Overall, the industry generates about €650 million annually, according to the Central Bureau of Statistics.

An intriguing place to view the action is Trompettersteeg, a metre-wide alley where the most desirable women are stationed. Look for the entrance in the block south of the Oude Kerk.

Clean Up

Over the past few years, city officials have reduced the number of windows in an effort to clean up the district. They claim it's not about morals but about crime: pimps, traffickers and money launderers have entered the scene and set the neighbourhood on a downward spiral. Opponents point to a growing local conservatism and say the government is using crime as an excuse, because it doesn't like Amsterdam's current reputation for sin. How far the city will take its clean-up efforts remains to be seen.

produce grown in its own garden plot. The slow-food credentials fused with gorgeous antique tableware add up to a rare bright spot in the dull Kalverstraat area. The full, sweet-and-savoury high tea is a scrumptious bonus. (☑320 41 32; www.gartine.nl; Taksteeg 7; mains €6-12, high tea €12-21; ☉10am-6pm Wed-Sun; ☂; ☒4/9/14/16/24/25 Spui)

Vleminckx

FRITES €

13 ✗ Map p26, B8

This hole-in-the-wall takeaway has drawn the hordes for its monumental *frites* since 1887. The standard is smothered in mayonnaise, though you can ask for ketchup, peanut sauce or a variety of spicy mayos. (Voetboogstraat

---

☑ Top Tip

Cafe vs Coffeeshop

There's a big difference between a cafe and a coffeeshop. To wit: 'cafe' means 'pub' throughout the Netherlands; a 'coffeeshop' is where one procures marijuana. The latter probably serves coffee, but the focus is on cannabis. Alcohol is not permitted.

On the other hand, cafes are cheery, beery local hangouts, where denizens spend hours reading, chatting with friends and snacking. Traditional brown cafes – named for the centuries of smoke stains on the walls – are the genre's crowning glory. Visiting one of these cosy, candlelit nirvanas is an Amsterdam must.

31; small/large €2.20/2.70, sauces €0.80; ☉11am-6pm Tue-Sat, to 7pm Thu, noon-6pm Sun & Mon; ☒1/2/5 Koningsplein)

Rob Wigboldus Vishandel

SANDWICH SHOP €

13 ✗ Map p26, B4

A wee three-table oasis in the midst of surrounding tourist tat, this fish shop in a tiny alley serves excellent herring sandwiches on a choice of crusty white or brown rolls. Don't like fish? Van den Berg's Broodjesbar (similar prices and hours), right next door, prepares a variety of other sandwiches, from a humble cheese-filled roll to *gehakt* (thin meatball slices served warm with killer-hot mustard). (☑626 33 88; Zoutsteeg 6; sandwiches €2.50-4.50; ☉breakfast & lunch; ☒4/9/16/24/25 Dam)

Thais Snackbar Bird

THAI €€

14 ✗ Map p26, E4

Don't tell the Chinese neighbours, but this is some of the best Asian food on the Zeedijk – the cooks, wedged in a tiny kitchen, don't skimp on lemongrass, fish sauce or chilli. The resulting curries and basil-laden meat and seafood dishes will knock your socks off. There's a bit more room to spread out in the (slightly pricier) restaurant across the street at No 72. (☑420 62 89; www.thai-bird.nl; Zeedijk 77; mains €9-15; ☉1-10pm; ☒4/9/16/24/25 Centraal Station)

D'Vijff Vlieghen
CONTEMPORARY DUTCH €€€

15 🍴 Map p26, A7

So what if every tourist and business visitor eats here? Sometimes the herd gets it right. 'The Five Flies' is a classic, spread out over five 17th-century canal houses. Old-wood dining rooms are full of character, featuring Delft tiles and works by Rembrandt and Breitner. Some chairs have brass plates for the celebrities who have sat in them. (📞530 40 60; www.vijffvlieghen.nl; Spuistraat 294-302; mains €26-33, set menus from €45.50; ⏲dinner; 🚊1/2/5 Spui)

'Skek
CAFE €€

16 🍴 Map p26, D3

Run by students (flashing your ID gets you one-third off), this friendly cafe-bar is an excellent place to get fat sandwiches on thick slices of multigrain bread, and healthy main dishes with chicken, fish or pasta. Bands occasionally perform at night (the bar stays open to 1am weekdays, and 3am on weekends). (📞427 05 51; www.skek.nl; Zeedijk 4-8; sandwiches €3-7, mains €12-14; ⏲noon-10pm; 📶; 🚊4/9/16/24/25 Centraal Station)

Lanskroon
BAKERY & SWEETS €

17 🍴 Map p26, A7

Other historic bakeries have prettier fixtures and daintier cakes, but only humble Lanskroon has such a remarkable *stroopwafel* – crispy, big as a dessert plate and slathered with caramel, honey or a deceptively healthy-tasting fig paste. In winter, locals come for spicy *speculaas* cookies and other holiday treats, and in summer there's thick nut- or fruit-swirled ice cream. (📞623 74 43; www.lanskroon.nl; Singel 385; items from €2; ⏲8am-5.30pm Mon-Fri, 9am-5.30pm Sat, 10am-5.30pm Sun; 👶; 🚊1/2/5 Spui)

Gebr Niemeijer
CAFE €

18 🍴 Map p26, C2

This French bakery is a real find amid the Nieuwendijk's head shops. Grab a newspaper and plop down at one of the sturdy wood tables to linger over flaky croissants for breakfast or fantastic sandwiches made with walnut bread and lamb sausage (or gruyére cheese, or fig jam…) for lunch. (www.gebroedersniemeijer.nl; Nieuwendijk 35; mains €4-8; ⏲8.15am-6.30pm Tue-Fri, to 5pm Sat, 9am-5pm Sun; 🚊1/2/5/13/17 Martelaarsgracht)

Haesje Claes
TRADITIONAL DUTCH €€

19 🍴 Map p26, A7

Haesje Claes' warm surrounds, a tad touristy but with lots of dark wood and antique knick-knacks, are just the place to sample comforting pea soup and *stamppot* (potatoes mashed with kale, endive or sauerkraut). The fish starter has a great sampling of different Dutch fish. (📞624 99 98; www.haesjeclaes.nl; Spuistraat 273-275; mains €16-25, set menus from €27.50; ⏲noon-10pm; 👶; 🚊1/2/5 Spui)

Local Life
Villa Zeezicht

While **Villa Zeezicht** (✆ 626 74 33; Torensteeg 7; mains €5-12; ⏱9am-9.30pm; 🚊1/2/5/13/14/17 Raadhuisstraat) serves decent sandwiches and pastas, it's really all just clumsy foreplay for the homemade *appeltaart* (apple pie), a deserved Amsterdam legend. Fork into a mountain of apples dusted in cinnamon, surrounded by warm pastry and fresh cream. In warm weather, tables are set up on the bridge over the Singel.

Hofje van Wijs   CAFE €

20 ❌ Map p26, E3

The 200-year-old coffee and tea vendor Wijs & Zonen (the Queen's purveyor) maintains this pretty courtyard cafe. In addition to the usual offerings (cakes!), it serves inexpensive Dutch stews plus local beers and liqueurs. (✆624 04 36; www.hofjevanwijs.nl; Zeedijk 43; mains €8.50-10.50; ⏱noon-6pm Tue-Fri & Sun, 10am-6pm Sat; 🚊4/9/16/24/25 Centraal Station)

Drinking

Wynand Fockink   TASTING HOUSE

21 🔵 Map p26, C5

This small tasting house (dating from 1679) serves scores of *jenever* and liqueurs in an arcade behind Grand Hotel Krasnapolsky. Although there are no seats or stools, it is an intimate place to knock back a taste or two with a friend. Guides give an English-language tour of the distillery every Saturday at 12.30pm (€9, reservations not required). (www.wynand-fockink.nl; Pijlsteeg 31; ⏱3-9pm; 🚊4/9/16/24/25 Dam)

Hoppe   BROWN CAFE

22 🔵 Map p26, A8

Boasting the city's highest beer turnover rate, gritty Hoppe has been filling glasses for more than 300 years. Journalists, bums, socialites and raconteurs toss back brews amid the ancient wood panelling. Most months the energetic crowd spews out from the dark interior and onto the Spui. Note the entrance is to the right of the pub-with-terrace of the same name. (www.cafehoppe.nl; Spui 18-20; 🚊1/2/5 Spui)

Café In 't Aepjen   BROWN CAFE

23 🔵 Map p26, E3

Candles burn even during the day at this bar based in a mid-16th-century house, which is one of two remaining wooden buildings in the city. Vintage jazz on the stereo enhances the time-warp feel. The name allegedly comes from the bar's role in the 16th and 17th centuries as a crash pad for sailors from the Far East, who often toted *aapjes* (monkeys) with them. (✆626 84 01; www.cafeintaepjen.nl; Zeedijk 1; 🚊4/9/16/24/25 Centraal Station)

Café Belgique
BEER CAFE

24 🎧 Map p26, B4

Pull up a stool at the carved wooden bar and make your choice from the glinting brass taps. It's all about Belgian beers here, as you may have surmised. Eight flow from the spouts, and 30 or so are available in bottles. The ambience is quintessential *gezellig* (cosy) and draws lots of chilled-out locals. There's live music and DJs some nights. (www.cafe-belgique.nl; Gravenstraat 2; ⊙from 2pm; 🚊4/9/16/24/25 Dam)

In de Olofspoort
BROWN CAFE

25 🎧 Map p26, D3

The door of this brown cafe–tasting room was once the city gate. It's a great place to go for more heady liqueurs after Wynand Fockink shuts. A crew of regulars has dedicated bottles stocked just for them. Check out the jaw-dropping selection behind the backroom bar. Occasional singalongs add to the atmosphere. (📞624 39 18; www.olofspoort.com; Nieuwebrugsteeg 13; ⊙from 4pm Wed & Thu, from 3pm Fri-Sun; 🚊4/9/16/24/25 Centraal Station)

't Mandje
BROWN CAFE

26 🎧 Map p26, E4

Amsterdam's oldest gay bar opened in 1927, then shut in 1982, when the Zeedijk grew too seedy. But its trinket-covered interior was lovingly dusted every week until it reopened in 2008. The devoted bartenders can tell you stories about the bar's brassy lesbian founder. It's one of the most *gezellig* places in the centre, gay or straight. (www.cafetmandje.nl; Zeedijk 63; ⊙closed Mon; 🚊4/9/16/24/25 Centraal Station)

Café de Barderij
BAR

27 🎧 Map p26, E3

This friendly, candlelit bar draws a mixture of local gay regulars and tourists. It has killer views of the canal out back and Zeedijk in front, making it a must on Queen's Day. Come on Mondays and Wednesdays when the bar serves a two-course homemade Dutch meal (€12.50) in the basement. A gay crowd flocks here on Sundays for free meatballs. (www.barderij.com; Zeedijk 14; 🚊4/9/16/24/25 Centraal Station)

Brouwerij De Prael
BEER CAFE

28 🎧 Map p26, D3

Sample organic beers named after classic Dutch singers at the multilevel tasting room of De Prael brewery, a do-good business known for employing people with a history of mental illness.

☑ Top Tip

How to Drink Jenever

You're at the local tasting house, and you've ordered a *jenever* (akin to gin). It arrives in a tulip-shaped shot glass filled to the brim. You can't pick it up without spilling it. What to do? Bend over the bar, with your hands behind your back, and take a deep sip. That's what tradition dictates.

It's mostly a younger crowd that hoists suds and forks into well-priced stews and other Dutch standards at the comfy couches and big wood tables strewn about. Bands plug in some nights. (📞408 44 69; www.deprael.nl; Oudezijds Armsteeg 26; ⏰11am-11pm Tue-Sun; 🚊4/9/16/24/25 Centraal Station)

Café de Jaren
GRAND CAFE

29 🚇 Map p26, C8

Watch the Amstel flow by from the balcony and waterside terraces of this soaring, bright and very grand cafe, one of our favourites. The great reading table has loads of foreign publications for whiling away hours over beers. If you're feeling a bit peckish, hit the fabulous buffet salad bar (a rarity in Amsterdam). (www.cafedejaren .nl; Nieuwe Doelenstraat 20; ⏰from 9.30am; 🚊4/9/14/16/24/25 Muntplein)

Getto
GAY BAR

30 🚇 Map p26, D4

This groovy, long restaurant-bar is loved for its open, welcoming attitude, great people-watching from the front, and a rear lounge where you can chill. It's a haven for the younger gay and lesbian crowd and anyone who wants a little bohemian subculture in the Red Light District's midst. The food is good and cheap, too. (www.getto.nl; Warmoesstraat 51; ⏰Tue-Sun; 🚊4/9/16/24/25 Centraal Station)

JULIET COOMBE / GETTY IMAGES ©

Sexmuseum Amsterdam (p30)

Entertainment

Bitterzoet
LIVE MUSIC, CLUB

31 ⭐ Map p26, C2

Always full, always changing, this is one of the friendliest venues in town. One night it might be full of skater dudes; the next, relaxed 30-somethings. Music (sometimes live, sometimes a DJ) can be funk, roots, drum'n'bass, Latin, Afrobeat, old-school jazz or hip-hop groove. (www.bitterzoet.com; Spuistraat 2; 🚋 1/2/5/13/17 Martelaarsgracht)

Winston Kingdom
LIVE MUSIC, CLUB

32 ⭐ Map p26, C4

This is a club that even nonclubbers will love for its indie-alternative music beats, smiling DJs and stage-diving cover bands. No matter what's on – from 'dubstep mayhem' to Elvis Costello punk tributes – the scene can get pretty wild in the good-time little space. (www.winston.nl; Warmoesstraat 127, Hotel Winston; 🚋 4/9/16/24/25 Dam)

Brug 9
JAZZ

33 ⭐ Map p26, A4

Brug means 'bridge' and that's where this atmospheric little venue resides: under the Torensluis, Amsterdam's oldest bridge. The makeshift, brick-walled cellar hosts exhibitions, film screenings and especially avant-garde jazz concerts; check the website for the schedule. Reach it by heading down the stairs by the bridge, opposite Singel 157 or 161. (www.brug9.nl; opposite Singel 157 or 161; 🚋 1/2/5/13/14/17 Raadhuisstraat)

Casa Rosso
SEX SHOW

34 ⭐ Map p26, D5

It might be stretching it to describe a live sex show as 'classy', but this theatre is clean and comfortable and always packed with couples and hen's-night parties. Acts can be male, female, both or lesbian (although not gay...sorry boys!). Performers demonstrate everything from positions of the Kama Sutra to pole dances and incredible tricks with lit candles. (www.casarosso.nl; Oudezijds Achterburgwal 106-108; admission with/without drinks €50/35; ⊘ 7pm-2am; 🚋 4/9/16/24/25 Dam)

Frascati
THEATRE

35 ⭐ Map p26, C7

This experimental theatre is a draw for young Dutch directors, choreo-graphers and producers. Expect multicultural dance and music performances, as well as hip hop, rap and breakdancing. Frascati hosts a theatre, dance, art and music festival, Breakin'Walls (www.breakinwalls.nl), in both November (main festival) and April (mini-festival). (☎ 626 68 66; www.theaterfrascati.nl; Nes 63; ⊘ closed Aug; 🚋 4/9/14/16/25 Rokin)

Casablanca
LIVE MUSIC

36 ⭐ Map p26, E3

Casablanca once had a hot reputation for jazz (combos still take the stage

Understand

The Smoking Lowdown

Despite what you may have heard, cannabis is not *technically* legal in the Netherlands – yet it is widely tolerated. Here's the deal: the possession and purchase of small amounts (5g) of 'soft drugs' (ie marijuana, hashish, space cakes and mushroom-based truffles) is allowed, and users aren't prosecuted for smoking or carrying this amount. This means that coffeeshops are actually conducting an illegal business – but again, it is tolerated to a certain extent. Though maybe not where foreigners are concerned...

Coffeeshops Going Up in Smoke?

In January 2013, new laws are set to go into effect that ban foreigners from toking up in Amsterdam's infamous coffeeshops. Only Dutch residents who have procured a one-year 'weed pass' will be able to purchase grass and hash. Far-right politicians initiated the legislation, citing gang-related crime and health risks associated with the industry. Amsterdammers have fought it, saying the law will just drive the trade underground.

The law went into effect as planned in May 2012 in the Netherlands' southern cities along the Belgian and German borders. At press time, it was wait-and-see as to whether it will be enforced in Amsterdam. A court case focussing on the issue of discrimination is pending. If the case fails, many coffeeshop owners say they will ignore the ban and hope Amsterdam city officials – who are against it – will close their eyes to the matter. But it won't be easy with national authorities harshing their high.

Dos & Don'ts (Just in Case)

If the coffeeshops remain open to foreigners, keep in mind the following:
▶ Whether it is grass or hash, and smoked, eaten or inhaled through a vaporiser, most visitors admit it's much stronger than what they are accustomed to. Ask the staff how much to take and heed their advice, even if nothing happens after an hour.

▶ Ask at the bar for the menu of goods on offer, usually packaged in small bags. You can also buy ready-made joints (€3 to €7) in nifty, reusable packaging. Most shops offer rolling papers, pipes or even bongs to use.

early in the week), but now it's better known as a karaoke madhouse on the weekends. Next door at No 24 is Casablanca Variété, a circus theatre where magicians and more take the stage (€7 cover charge). (www.cafecasablanca .nl; Zeedijk 26; 🚊4/9/16/24/25 Centraal Station)

De Brakke Grond THEATRE

37 ⭐ Map p26, C6

De Brakke Grond sponsors a fantastic array of music, experimental video, modern dance and exciting, young Flemish theatre at its performance hall. (📞626 68 66; www.brakkegrond.nl; Nes 45, Flemish Cultural Centre; 🚊4/9/14/16/25 Rokin)

Shopping

Condomerie Het Gulden Vlies SPECIALITY SHOP

38 🔒 Map p26, C5

This is where the well-dressed johnson shops for variety. Perfectly positioned for the Red Light District, the boutique stocks hundreds of types of condoms (including the Coripa brand, which comes in 55 sizes), lubricants and saucy gifts. Some of the novelty condoms may remind you of your favourite cartoon character. (www.condomerie.nl; Warmoesstraat 141; 🚊4/9/16/24/25 Dam)

American Book Center BOOKS

39 🔒 Map p26, A7

The excellent three-storey shop is the biggest source of English-language books in Amsterdam. Its greatest strengths are in the artsy ground-floor department, but on the upper floors there's fiction and oodles of special-interest titles, plus a good travel section. It also stocks foreign periodicals such as the *New York Times*. (www.abc .nl; Spui 12; ⏰11am-8pm Mon, from 10am Tue-Sat, 11am-6.30pm Sun; 🚊1/2/5 Spui)

PGC Hajenius SPECIALITY SHOP

40 🔒 Map p26, B7

Even if you're not a cigar connoisseur, this tobacco emporium is worth a browse. Inside is all art deco stained glass, gilt trim and soaring ceilings.

Top Tip

Magic Truffles

Psilocybin mushrooms are banned in the Netherlands, but trippy magic truffles are legal. They're widely available at 'smart shops', which deal in organic uppers and natural hallucinogens. Counter staff advise on the nuances of dosages and possible effects, as if at a pharmacy. Listen to them. Every year, emergency-room nurses have to sit with people on bad trips brought on by consuming more than the recommended amount. Also, it seems obvious, but never buy truffles or other drugs on the street.

Regular customers, including members of the Dutch royal family, have private humidors here. You can sample your Cuban stogie or other exotic purchases in the handsome smoking lounge. (www.hajenius.com; Rokin 96; 🚊4/9/14/16/24/25 Spui)

Hemp Works   CLOTHING, ACCESSORIES

41 🔒 Map p26, C2

Hemp Works carries a big selection of eco-friendly clothing and bags, all made with organic hemp, cotton and bamboo. The locally made Dutch items sell under the label Hemp Hoodlamb. Some of the clothes have special touches like hidden pockets for your stash. (www.hempworks.nl; Nieuwendijk 13; 🚊1/2/5/13/17 Martelaarsgracht)

Kokopelli   SMART DRUGS

42 🔒 Map p26, D3

Were it not for its truffles trade you might swear this large, beautiful space was a fashionable clothing or homewares store. In addition to smart drugs, there's a coffee and juice bar and a chill-out lounge area overlooking Damrak. (www.kokopelli.nl; Warmoesstraat 12; ⏰11am-10pm; 🚊4/9/16/24/25 Centraal Station)

Absolute Danny   EROTICA

43 🔒 Map p26, D5

Named by Dutch *Playboy* as Amsterdam's classiest sex shop, Absolute Danny specialises in fetish clothing, lingerie and leather, along with hard-core videos and dildos just for fun. (www.absolutedanny.com; Oudezijds Achterburgwal 78; ⏰11am-9pm Mon-Sat, from noon Sun; 🚊4/9/16/24/25 Dam)

De Bijenkorf   DEPARTMENT STORE

44 🔒 Map p26, B5

The city's most fashionable department store is in the highest-profile location, facing the Royal Palace. Design-conscious shoppers will enjoy the well-chosen clothing, toys, household accessories and books. It has a small restaurant or snack bar and a bathroom (€0.50) on each floor. The snazzy cafe on the 5th floor has a terrace with steeple views. (www.de bijenkorf.nl; Dam 1; 🚊4/9/16/24/25 Dam)

ANNEMARIE BAURDOUX / HEMP WORKS ©

Hemp Works

Hema
DEPARTMENT STORE

45 🔒 Map p26, C4

What used to be the nation's equivalent of Marks & Spencer, Woolworths or Target now attracts as many design aficionados as bargain hunters. Expect low prices, reliable quality and a wide range of products, including good-value wines and delicatessen goods. There's another branch at the Kalvertoren shopping centre (Kalverstraat 212). (www.hema.nl; Nieuwendijk 174; 🚊4/9/16/24/25 Dam)

Mr B
EROTICA

46 🔒 Map p26, D4

Kinky! The tamer wares at this renowned Red Light District shop for guys include leather and rubber suits, hoods and bondage equipment, all made to measure if you want. It also pierces and tattoos. (www.misterb.com; Warmoesstraat 89; ⏰10am-6.30pm Mon-Wed & Fri, 10am-9pm Thu, 11am-6pm Sat, 1-6pm Sun; 🚊4/9/16/24/25 Dam)

Laundry Industry
CLOTHING

47 🔒 Map p26, B7

Hip, urban types head here for well-cut, well-designed women's clothes by this Dutch design house. Minimalist, functional fashion in neutrals, but with attractive details like pintucking, are the claim to fame. There are a couple of other branches around town, but the Spui location is the main shop. (www.laundryindustry.com; Spui 1; 🚊4/9/14/16/24/25 Spui)

Explore

Jordaan & Western Canals

If Amsterdam's neighbourhoods held a 'best personality' contest, the Jordaan would surely win. Its intimacy is contagious, with jovial bar singalongs, beery brown cafes and flower-box-adorned eateries spilling out onto the narrow streets. The Western Canals flow next door. Grand old buildings and oddball little speciality shops line the glinting waterways. Roaming around them can cause days to vanish.

YADID LEVY / GETTY IMAGES ©

The Sights in a Day

☼ Do the Dutch thing and carve into a hulking pancake at, well, **Pancakes!** (p53). Poke around the surrounding shops, then cross over Prinsengracht to see what life on the water is like at the **Houseboat Museum** (p51).

☼ Devote the afternoon to the neighbourhood's gorgeous canals. Visit **Het Grachtenhuis** (p50), which tells the story of the 400-year-old waterways and their engineering genius. Afterward walk along the Herengracht and ogle the Golden Age manors rising up along the canal. No wonder the entire area is a Unesco World Heritage site. Munch a canalside lunch at **Buffet van Odette** (p54). Photography buffs can see what's on at **Huis Marseille** (p51).

☾ Head over to the **Anne Frank Huis** (p44) in the early evening, when crowds are thinnest. For dinner, sip Spanish sparkling wine while rounds of tapas hit the table at **La Oliva** (p54). Then take your pick of brown cafes for a nightcap. **Café 't Smalle** (p56) always hosts a high-spirited group. Or croon with the crowd at **De Twee Zwaantjes** (p57).

For a local's day in the Jordaan and Western Canals, see p46.

◉ Top Sights
Anne Frank Huis (p44)

○ Local Life
Shopping the Jordaan & Western Canals (p46)

♥ Best of Amsterdam

Eating
Moeders (p54)

Drinking
De Twee Zwaantjes (p57)

Café 't Smalle (p56)

Shopping
Noordermarkt (p47)

Frozen Fountain (p61)

Museums & Galleries
Het Grachtenhuis (p50)

Houseboat Museum (p51)

Getting There

🚋 **Tram** For the Western Canals, trams 13, 14 and 17 drop off near the shops and top sights; trams 1, 2 and 5 to the Spui are also just a short walk away. For the Jordaan, tram 10 along Marnixstraat is your best bet for the neighbourhood's western edge; trams 13 and 14 along Rozengracht go through the centre.

Top Sights
Anne Frank Huis

It is one of the 20th century's most compelling stories: a young Jewish girl forced into hiding with her family and their friends to escape deportation by the Nazis. The house they used as a hideaway attracts nearly one million visitors every year. Walking through the bookcase-door of the 'Secret Annexe' and into the claustrophobic living quarters is to step back into a time that seems both distant and tragically real.

Anne Frank House

◉ Map p48, C4

www.annefrank.org

Prinsengracht 276

adult/child €9/free

⏰ 9am-7pm mid-Sep–mid-Mar, to 9pm Sat, longer hours in summer

🚊 13/14/17 Westermarkt

Anne Frank's famous diary

Don't Miss

The Occupants

The Franks – father Otto, mother Edith, older sister Margot and Anne – moved into the hidden chambers in July 1942, along with Mr and Mrs van Pels (whom Anne called the van Daans in her diary) and their son Peter. Five months later Fritz Pfeffer (aka Albert van Dussel) joined the household. The group lived there until they were mysteriously betrayed to the Gestapo in August 1944.

Offices & Warehouse

The building originally held Otto Frank's pectin (a substance used in jelly-making) business. On the lower floors you'll see the former offices of Victor Kugler, Otto's business partner; and the desks of Miep Gies, Bep Voskuijl and Jo Kleiman, three women who worked in the office and provided food, clothing and other goods for the household.

Secret Annexe

The upper floors in the *achterhuis* (rear house) contain the Secret Annexe, where the living quarters have been preserved in powerful austerity. As you enter Anne's small bedroom, you can still sense the remnants of a young girl's dreams: view the photos of Hollywood stars and postcards of the Dutch Royal family she pasted on the wall.

The Diary

More haunting exhibits and videos await after you return to the front house – including Anne's red-plaid diary itself, sitting alone in its glass case. Watch the video of Anne's old schoolmate Hanneli Gosler, who describes encountering Anne at Bergen-Belsen. Read heartbreaking letters from Otto, the only Secret Annexe occupant to survive the concentration camps.

☑ **Top Tips**

▶ Come after 6pm to avoid the biggest crowds. Queues can easily be an hour-plus wait otherwise.

▶ Buying tickets in advance allows you to skip the queue and enter via a separate door (left of the main entrance).

▶ Prebook two ways: via the website (€0.50 surcharge), though you must buy the tickets several days ahead of time and be able to print them; or via the tourist information office at Centraal Station (€1 surcharge), which you can do on shorter notice. Both methods give you a set time for entry.

▶ Download 'Anne's Amsterdam', a free app available in Dutch, English and German.

✕ **Take a Break**

The museum cafe offers apple pie and canal views. For pancakes, sandwiches and 18th-century atmosphere aplenty, stroll over to Café 't Smalle (p56).

Local Life
Shopping the Jordaan & Western Canals

These are Amsterdam's prime neighbourhoods to stumble upon offbeat little shops selling items you'd find nowhere else. Velvet ribbons? Herb-spiced Gouda? Vintage jewellery? They're all here amid the Western Canals' quirky stores and the Jordaan's eclectic boutiques and markets. Everything is squashed into a grid of tiny lanes – a perfect place in which to lose yourself for an afternoon stroll.

....

1 Antiquing at De Looier

Anyone who likes peculiar old stuff might enter **De Looier Antiques Centre** (www.antiekcentrumamsterdam.nl; Elandsgracht 109; ⏰11am-6pm Mon & Wed-Fri, to 5pm Sat & Sun; 🚊7/10/17 Elandsgracht), a knick-knack minimall, and never come out. You're just as likely to find 1940s silk dresses as you are

1970s Swedish porn. Brasserie Blazer serves well-priced French fare inside to fuel the browsing.

❷ Tunes at Johnny Jordaanplein

The small square **Johnny Jordaanplein** (cnr Prinsengracht & Elandsgracht; 🚊13/14/17 Westermarkt) is dedicated to the local hero and singer of schmaltzy tunes such as *Bij ons in de Jordaan* (We in the Jordaan). There are bronze busts of Johnny and his band, but the real star here is the colourful utility hut splashed with nostalgic lyrics.

❸ Wander the Negen Straatjes

The **Negen Straatjes** (Nine Streets; www.de9straatjes.nl) comprise a tic-tac-toe board of wee shops dealing in vintage fashions, housewares and oddball specialities from toothbrushes to antique eyeglass frames. It's bounded by Reestraat, Hartenstraat and Gasthuismolensteeg to the north and Runstraat, Huidenstraat and Wijde Heisteeg to the south. Bonus points if you find the doll doctor!

❹ Munch at Lunchcafe Nielsen

Looking for where the locals go to lunch and brunch in the Negen Straatjes? **Lunchcafe Nielsen** (📞330 60 06; Berenstraat 19; mains €5-10; ⊙8am-4pm Mon-Fri, to 6pm Sat, 9am-5pm Sun; 🚊13/14/17 Westermarkt) it is. Under leafy murals, chow on speciality quiches, salads, and fresh lemon and apple cakes that disappear as quickly as they're put out.

❺ Rummage the Noordermarkt

The **Noordermarkt** (Northern Market; Noorderkerkplein; www.boerenmarktamsterdam.nl; ⊙8am-2pm Mon, 9am-4pm Sat; 🚊3 Nieuwe Willemsstraat) surrounds the Noorderkerk and hosts two bazaars. On Monday mornings it's a trove of secondhand clothing (great rummage piles) and assorted antique trinkets. On Saturdays, most (but not all) of the clothing stalls are replaced by gorgeous produce and *kaas* (cheese) from growers around Amsterdam.

❻ Get Hip on Haarlemmerdijk

The street **Haarlemmerdijk** buzzes with stylish shops and lots of places to snack or unwind over a drink. It is fast becoming a culinary destination, not just for restaurants but for its slew of gourmet provisions and kitchen shops. Keep an eye out for chocolatiers, cookbook vendors and tea emporiums among the retailers.

❼ Relax at De Kat in de Wijngaert

A brown cafe that exudes overwhelming *gezelligheid*, **De Kat in de Wijngaert** (📞620 45 54; Lindengracht 160; 🚊3 Nieuwe Willemsstraat) is the kind of place where one beer soon turns to half a dozen – maybe it's the influence of the old-guard arts types who hang out here. Try soaking it up with what many people vote as the best *tosti* (toasted sandwich) in town.

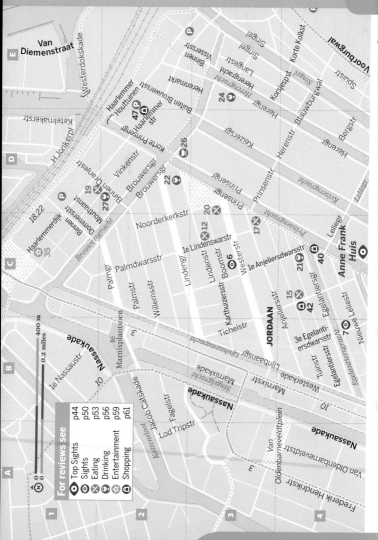

For reviews see
Top Sights	p44
Sights	p50
Eating	p53
Drinking	p56
Entertainment	p59
Shopping	p61

0.2 miles
400 m

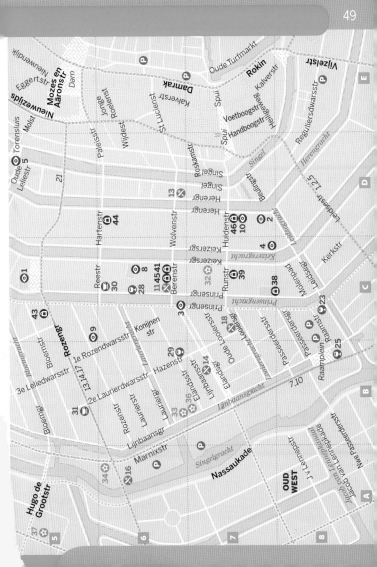

Sights

Westerkerk

CHURCH

1 Map p48, C5

This blue-crowned Protestant church, built in 1631, has become a symbol of the Jordaan. To be a true local, it's said, you must be born within earshot of the Westerkerk's carillon bells. Rembrandt supposedly lies here, in an unmarked pauper's grave. Climbing the 85m-high tower (by tour only) reveals striking canal views, but it's steep and claustrophobic – not for the faint-hearted. (Western Church; ☎624 77 66; www.westerkerk.nl; Prinsengracht 281; church admission free, tower €7; ☼church 11am-3pm Mon-Fri Apr-Sep, also Sat Jul & Aug, tower 10am-5.30pm Mon-Fri, to 7.30pm Sat Apr-Sep; ◻13/14/17 Westermarkt)

Het Grachtenhuis

MUSEUM

2 Map p48, D7

If you're intrigued by the Canal Ring and what a feat of engineering it is, don't miss the Canal House, which explains how the waterways and the houses that line them became an integral part of Amsterdam city planning. A 40-minute audio tour guides you through. Entry is via timed tickets; reserve online in advance (which also provides a discount). (Canal House; www.hetgrachtenhuis.nl; Herengracht 386; adult/child €12/6; ☼10am-5pm Tue-Sun; ◻1/2/5 Spui)

Miniature canal houses, Het Grachtenhuis

ALBERTO PAREDES / ALAMY ©

Houseboat Museum

MUSEUM

3   Map p48, C6

The quirky Houseboat Museum, a 23m-long sailing barge from 1914, offers a good sense of how cosy life can be on the water. The actual displays are minimal, but you can watch a slide show of eye-popping boats, and inspect the sleeping, living, cooking and dining quarters on board. In case you were wondering: most vessels have sewerage hook-ups. (427 07 50; www.houseboatmuseum.nl; Prinsengracht, opposite 296; adult/child €3.75/3; 11am-5pm Tue-Sun Mar-Oct, 11am-5pm Fri-Sun Nov-Feb, closed Jan; 13/14/17 Westermarkt)

Huis Marseille

MUSEUM

4   Map p48, C7

This well-curated photography museum stages large-scale, temporary exhibitions by international artists. Themes might include portraiture, nature or regional photography. The gallery space spreads over several floors of a historic home and spills into a tiny summer house in the garden. There's a terrific little library, too. (www.huismarseille.nl; Keizersgracht 401; adult/child €5/free; 11am-6pm Tue-Sun; 1/2/5 Keizersgracht)

Reypenaer Cheese Tasting

CULINARY

5   Map p48, D5

Here's your chance to become a *kaas* connoisseur. The 100-plus-year-old Dutch cheesemaker Reypenaer offers tastings in a rustic classroom under its shop. The hour-long session (available in English) includes six cheeses plus optional wine and port pairings. The staff leads you through them from young to old, helping you to appreciate each hunk's look, smell and taste. Call for the schedule. (320 63 33; www.reypenaer.com; Singel 182; tastings from €10; 1/2/5/13/17 Raadhuisstraat)

Pianola Museum

MUSEUM

6   Map p48, C3

This is a very special place, crammed with pianolas from the early 1900s, as well as nearly 20,000 music rolls. Every month (except July and August) player-piano concerts are held, featuring anything from Mozart to Fats Waller and rare classical or jazz tunes composed especially for the instrument. The curator gives demonstrations with great zest. (627 96 24; www.pianola.nl; Westerstraat 106; adult/child €5/3; 2-5pm Sun; 3/10 Marnixplein)

Electric Ladyland

MUSEUM

7   Map p48, B4

The world's first museum of fluorescence is a hippie-trippy treat. Even if you didn't eat a space cake before arriving, you're gonna feel like it, as grey-ponytailed artist and owner Nick Padalino takes you to his shop's basement and shows you all kinds of glow-in-the-dark objects, from psychedelic sculptures to luminescent rocks. Allow a good hour for the tour. (www.electric-lady-land.com; 2e Leliedwarsstraat 5;

Understand

Canals

History

In Dutch a canal is a *gracht* (pronounced '*khrakht*'), and the main canals form the central *grachtengordel* (canal ring). The beauties came to life in the early 1600s, after Amsterdam's population grew beyond its medieval walls, and city planners put together an ambitious design for expansion. Far from being simply decorative or picturesque, or even just waterways for transport, the canals were necessary to drain and reclaim the waterlogged land.

Core Canals

Starting from the core, the major semicircular canals are the Singel, Herengracht, Keizersgracht and Prinsengracht. An easy way to remember them is that, apart from the singular **Singel** (which originally was a moat that defended Amsterdam's outer limits), these canals are in alphabetical order.

The **Herengracht** is where Amsterdam's wealthiest residents moved once the canals were completed. They named the waterway after the Heeren XVII (17 Gentlemen) of the Dutch East India Company, and built their mansions alongside it. Almost as swanky was the **Keizersgracht** (Emperor's Canal), a nod to Holy Roman Emperor Maximilian I. The **Prinsengracht** – named after William the Silent, Prince of Orange and the first Dutch royal – was designed as a slightly cheaper canal with smaller residences and warehouses. It also acted as a barrier against the crusty working-class quarter beyond, aka the Jordaan. Today the Prinsengracht is the liveliest of Amsterdam's inner canals, with cafes, shops and houseboats lining the quays.

Radial Canals

The three major radial canals cut across the core canals like spokes on a bicycle. The **Brouwersgracht** – aka the 'Brewers Canal' – is one of Amsterdam's most beautiful waterways. It takes its name from the many breweries that lined the banks in the 16th and 17th centuries. The **Leidsegracht** was named after the city of Leiden, to which it was the main water route. Peaceful **Reguliersgracht** was named after an order of monks whose monastery was located nearby.

In 2010 Unesco dubbed the 400-year-old waterways a World Heritage site. The Jordaan & Western Canals neighbourhood is a prime place to watch them float by.

adult/child €5/free; ⊘2-5pm Tue-Sat;
🚊13/14/17 Westermarkt)

Netherlands Media
Art Institute   CULTURAL BUILDING

8 ◉ Map p48, C6

From the hilarious and ridiculous to
the deep and experimental, there's always something interesting in NMAI's
changing exhibits. Don't expect to
see works by the hitmakers or TV
directors of tomorrow, though. The
institute is specifically about video as
art. Works are displayed in a warren
of canal-house rooms. Prepare to have
your mind expanded at every turn.
(www.nimk.nl; Keizersgracht 264; adult/stu-
dent €4.50/2.50; ⊘11am-5pm Tue-Fri, 1-5pm
Sat & Sun; 🚊13/14/17 Westermarkt)

Stedelijk Museum
Bureau Amsterdam   MUSEUM

9 ◉ Map p48, C5

Don't blink or you might walk right
past this unobtrusive outpost, a
'project space' of the Stedelijk Museum. Exhibits here – from painting and
sculpture to new media and installa-
tion pieces – present contemporary
artists whose work reflects Amsterdam culture. Shows change about
every two weeks; ring to make sure it's
not closed while exhibitions are being
changed. (☎422 04 71; www.smba.nl;
Rozenstraat 59; admission free; ⊘11am-5pm
Tue-Sun; 🚊13/14/17 Westermarkt)

Bijbels Museum   MUSEUM

10 ◉ Map p48, D7

Not just a museum of Bibles, this
canal-house trove is more like a
museum about the Bible's importance
in 19th-century culture. It contains
musty mummies, hand-carved models
of the Tabernacle and the Temple in
Jerusalem, as well as several antique
Bibles (check out the 1477 Delft edition). Near the pretty garden, there's
also a display of biblical smells (nicer
than it sounds). (Bible Museum; www.bij
belsmuseum.nl; Herengracht 366-368; adult/
child €8/4; ⊘10am-5pm Mon-Sat, 11am-5pm
Sun; 🚊1/2/5 Spui)

Eating

Pancakes!   TRADITIONAL DUTCH €

11 ✕ Map p48, C6

Just as many locals as tourists grace
the blue-tile tables at snug little
Pancakes!, carving into all the usual
options, plus daily creations like ham,
chicory and cheese or chicken curry
pancakes. The batter is made with
flour sourced from a local mill. (www
.pancakesamsterdam.com; Berenstraat
38; pancakes €6-10; ⊘10am-7pm; 🖐;
🚊13/14/17 Westermarkt)

Koevoet   ITALIAN €€

12 ✕ Map p48, C3

The congenial Italian owners of
Koevoet took over a former cafe on
a quiet sidestreet, left the *gezellig*

decor untouched and started cooking up their home-country staples. Don't miss its signature drinkable dessert, *sgroppino limone*: sorbet, vodka and prosecco whisked at your table and poured into a champagne flute. (📞624 08 46; Lindenstraat 17; mains €12-23; ⏱dinner Tue-Sun; 🖊; 🚊3 Nieuwe Willemsstraat)

Buffet van Odette
CAFE €€

13 🍴 Map p48, D6

It's hard to get a seat in this tiny place on the weekend – it's packed with customers noshing on fat meatloaf sandwiches and omelettes with truffle cheese. Stay for sweets too: the sticky toffee and carrot cakes are delicious. Grab a seat by the window for one of the city's loveliest canal views. (www.buffet-amsterdam.nl; Herengracht 309; mains €8-16; ⏱10am-8.30pm Wed-Sat, to 5pm Sun & Mon; 🖊; 🚊1/2/5 Spui)

Balthazar's Keuken
MEDITERRANEAN €€

14 🍴 Map p48, B7

Balthazar's offers a fixed-price, three-course menu that changes weekly. With an open kitchen and only a few tables, it feels like eating at someone's house. It is consistently one of Amsterdam's top-rated restaurants, but don't expect a wide-ranging selection. The byword is basically 'whatever we have on hand' – and it's usually delectable. Reservations recommended. (📞420 21 14; www.balthazarskeuken.nl; Elandsgracht 108; 3-course menu €29.50; ⏱dinner Wed-Sat; 🚊7/10/17 Elandsgracht)

La Oliva
SPANISH €€

15 🍴 Map p48, C4

La Oliva's visually stunning food is inspired by the Basque region. Stroll by and you can see the colourful *pintxos* (tapas with a northern Spanish/southern French twist) skewered with wooden sticks and stacked on the gleaming bar. Hungry foodies sip *cava* (Spanish sparkling wine) and gaze lustfully at the stuffed figs, mushroom Manchego tartlets and Iberian ham with pear. (www.laoliva.nl; Egelantiersstraat 122-124; mains €21-26; ⏱lunch & dinner; 🚊3/10 Marnixplein)

Moeders
TRADITIONAL DUTCH €€

16 🍴 Map p48, A6

When 'Mothers' opened more than 25 years ago, staff asked customers to bring their own plates and photos of their mums as donations, and the result is still a delightful hotchpotch. So is the food, including *stamppot* (potatoes mashed with veggies and served with smoked sausage), seafood and a *rijsttafel*-style presentation of traditional Dutch dishes in many small plates. Book ahead. (📞626 79 57; www.moeders.com; Rozengracht 251; mains €15-19, 3-course menus €25-30; ⏱5pm-midnight Mon-Fri, noon-midnight Sat & Sun; 🖊; 🚊10/13/14/17 Marnixstraat)

Hostaria
ITALIAN €€

Located near La Oliva (see **15** 🍴 Map p48, C4) on a street bursting with excellent food, the Tuscan classics, fresh stuffed

Café 't Smalle (p56)

pastas and sublime yet simple desserts here are among our favourites. We witnessed a diner so thrilled with her ravioli that she asked to kiss the chef; he graciously complied. (📞420 21 14; 2e Egelantiersdwarsstraat 9; mains €13-26; 🕐dinner Tue-Sun; 🚊3/10 Marnixplein)

De Bolhoed
VEGETARIAN €€

17 ❌ Map p48, C3

The art-walled, bright-hued interior is a nice setting to tuck into enormous, organic Mexican-, Asian- and Italian-inspired dishes. Vegetarians swear by it. In warm weather there's a verdant little canalside terrace. Remember to leave some room for the banana-cream pie. (📞626 18 03; Prinsengracht 60-62; mains €13-15, 3-course menu €22; 🕐lunch & dinner; 📷; 🚊13/14/17 Westermarkt)

Festina Lente
CAFE €

18 ❌ Map p48, C7

This canalside neighbourhood hangout offers typical Jordaan *gezelligheid*, packed with regulars playing board games, reading poetry and snacking on small-portion Mediterranean dishes and big, crusty *broodjes* (sandwiches). (www.cafefestinalente.nl; Looiersgracht 40b; sandwiches €4-8, small plates €5-10; 🕐noon-10.30pm Sun & Mon, from 10.30am Tue-Sat; 📷)

Small World Catering

INTERNATIONAL €

19 ✕ Map p48, D1

It's no secret the carrot cake here has been known to spawn serious addictions, leading to impulsive bike rides across town to score a fix before closing time. If the cake isn't reason enough to come, the friendly international staff serves up daily specials like Aussie beef pie and ricotta cannelloni, along with killer sandwiches (try the pesto melt). (www.smallworldcatering .nl; Binnen Oranjestraat 14; mains €7-10; ⏰10.30am-7pm Tue-Sat, noon-6pm Sun; ✒; ₪3 Haarlemmerplein)

Winkel

CAFE €

20 ✕ Map p48, D3

This sprawling, indoor-outdoor space is great for people-watching, popular for coffees and small meals, and out-of-the-park for its tall, cakey apple pie.

Local Life
Wil Graanstra Friteshuis

Legions of Amsterdammers swear by the crispy spuds at **Wil Graanstra Friteshuis** (☎624 40 71; Westermarkt 11; frites €2-3.75; ⏰11am-6pm Mon-Sat). The family-run business has been frying by the Westerkerk since 1956. Most locals top their coneful with mayonnaise, though *oorlog* (a peanut sauce–mayo combo), curry sauce and *picalilly* (relish) rock the tastebuds, too.

On market days (Monday and Saturday) there's almost always a queue out the door. (www.winkel43.nl; Noordermarkt 43; mains €4-14; ⏰breakfast, lunch & dinner; ✒; ₪3 Nieuwe Willemsstraat)

Drinking

Café 't Smalle

BROWN CAFE

21 🚊 Map p48, C4

There's no more-convivial spot than this canalside terrace on a sunny day, and the romantic 18th-century interior is perfect in winter. Proof of its powerful *gezelligheid*, 't Smalle remains a lively local place even while being gushed over in multiple guidebooks. The antique porcelain beer pumps, lead-framed windows and other decor are so charming the bar has been reproduced in Japan. (www.t-smalle.nl; Egelantiersgracht 12; ⏰from 10am; ₪13/14/17 Westermarkt)

Finch

DESIGNER BAR

22 🚊 Map p48, D2

This funkalicious bar with its retro decor (deliberately mismatched yet somehow harmonious) is just the spot to hang out and knock back a few beers after a visit to the Noordermarkt. It's known for an arty-designy clientele and is always packed on the weekends. (☎626 24 61; Noordermarkt 5; ₪3 Nieuwe Willemsstraat)

De Pieper
BROWN CAFE

23 🚇 Map p48, C8

Considered by many to be the king of the brown cafes, De Pieper is small, unassuming and unmistakably old (built in 1665). The interior features stained-glass windows, fresh sand on the floors and antique Delft beer mugs hanging from the bar. It's a sweet place for sipping a late-night Wieckse Witte as you marvel at the claustrophobia of the low-ceilinged environs. (Prinsengracht 424; 🚋7/10 Raamplein)

't Arendsnest
BEER CAFE

24 🚇 Map p48, E3

Cosy 't Arendsnest stocks only Dutch beers, which are too often overshadowed by Belgian ones on local menus. The bartenders are evangelistic about the options from more than 50 breweries, including many small and hard-to-find suds makers – ask for the staff's expert recommendations. (www.arendsnest.nl; Herengracht 90; ⏱from 4pm Mon-Fri, from 2pm Sat & Sun; 🚋1/2/5/13/17 Nieuwezijds Kolk)

Café de Koe
BAR

25 🚇 Map p48, B8

'The Cow' is loved for its homey *gezellig* atmosphere, fun pop quizzes, darts tournaments, good (cheap) restaurant and free performances by local rock bands. A down-to-earth neighbourhood crowd swills beers upstairs by the funky cow mosaic, while diners

🔍 Local Life
De Twee Zwaantjes
To experience the Jordaan's famous (or infamous) tradition of drunken singalongs, duck into **De Twee Zwaantjes** (www.detweezwaantjes.nl; Prinsengracht 114; ⏱from 3pm; 🚋13/14/17 Westermarkt). The brown cafe is at its hilarious best on weekend nights, when crooners with big hair and ruffled shirts belt out nostalgic anthems, accompanied by accordions. Karaoke replaces the pros in summer.

below gather around worn wooden tables and order comfort food. Come for Sunday movie nights, or just to play board games. (www.cafedekoe.nl; Marnixstraat 381; 🚋7/10 Raamplein)

Café Tabac
CAFE

26 🚇 Map p48, D2

Is Café Tabac a brown cafe, a designer bar or simply an effortlessly cool place at which you can while away a few blissful hours at the intersection of two of Amsterdam's most stunning canals? The regulars don't seem concerned about definitions, so just enjoy the graceful views and kick back under the high-beamed ceilings to cool rock tunes. (www.cafetabac.eu; 2e Brouwersgracht 101; ⏱from 11am Sat-Mon, from 4pm Tue-Fri; 🚋3 Nieuwe Willemsstraat)

Vesper Bar

DESIGNER BAR

27 Map p48, D2

Rather than feeling totally out of place in the Jordaan, this luxe cocktail bar only gains a certain ineffable mystique by its location on a low-key stretch of Jordaanian shops and businesses. The cocktails will coax out your inner James Bond – or Vesper Lynd (the name of the Bond girl from *Casino Royale*). (☎420 45 92; www.vesperbar.nl; Vinkenstraat 57; ⊙from 8pm Tue-Thu, from 5pm Fri & Sat; ⛴3 Haarlemmerplein)

Café Restaurant van Puffelen

GRAND CAFE

28 Map p48, C6

Sprawling Van Puffelen, popular among cashed-up professionals and intellectual types, has lots of nooks and crannies for nice, cosy drinks and big, communal tables for sharing meals like antipasto and large salads.

(www.restaurantvanpuffelen.com; Prinsengracht 377; ⊙from 3pm Mon-Thu, from 1pm Fri, from noon Sat & Sun; ⛴13/14/17 Westermarkt)

Saarein

GAY & LESBIAN

29 Map p48, B6

A one-time feminist stronghold, Saarein is still a meeting place for lesbians, although these days gay men are welcome too. The cafe dates from the 1600s and vestiges remain. There's a small menu with tapas, soups and specials. (Elandsstraat 119; ⊙from 4pm Tue-Fri & Sun, from noon Sat; ⛴7/10/17 Elandsgracht)

Koffiehuis De Hoek

CAFE

30 Map p48, C6

De Hoek is a charming, old-fashioned *koffiehuis* (espresso bar) – not to be confused with a coffeeshop (where one procures pot). *Lekker* (tasty)

Understand
Gezelligheid

This particularly Dutch quality is one of the best reasons to visit Amsterdam. It's variously translated as snug, friendly, cosy, informal, companionable and convivial, but *gezelligheid* – the state of being *gezellig* – is something more easily experienced than defined. There's a sense of time stopping, an intimacy of the here and now that leaves all your troubles behind, at least until tomorrow. You can get the warm and fuzzy feeling in many places and situations: while nursing a brew with friends, over coffee and cake with neighbours, or lingering after a meal (the Dutch call this *natafelen*, or, in Dutch, 'after-table-ing'). Nearly any cosy establishment lit by candles probably qualifies. Old brown cafes, such as Café 't Smalle (p56) and De Pieper (p57), practically have *gezelligheid* on tap.

Koffiehuis De Hoek

breakfasts, sandwiches and cakes supplement the heavy-hitting java. (☎625 38 72; www.koffiehuisamsterdam.nl; Prinsengracht 341; ◷7.30am-4pm Tue-Fri, 9am-3.30pm Sat; 🚊13/14/17 Westermarkt)

Struik
CAFE

31 🚇 Map p48, B5

If you prefer your beer with a background of hip hop, breakbeats and soul, come to this graffitied corner cafe, which does good food (including a daily special for €7.50) then segues into a spot for drinking and chatting along to an old-school playlist or a DJ on weekends. (☎625 48 63; Rozengracht 160; ◷from 5pm Mon, from 11am Tue-Sat, from noon Sun; 🚊10/13/14/17 Marnixstraat)

Entertainment

Felix Meritis
ARTS CENTRE

32 ⭐ Map p48, C7

This wonderful arts and culture space hosts experimental theatre, music and dance performances, as well as lectures on politics, art and literature. The cafe here, with its huge open windows and clever outdoor seating (you'll see) overlooking the canal, is particularly great. 2013 marks the centre's 225th birthday with a slew of special events. (www.felix.meritis.nl; Keizersgracht 324, Felix Meritis Bldg; 🚊13/14/17 Westermarkt)

Understand
Dutch Design

Dutch design has a reputation for minimalist, creative approaches to everyday products, with a dose of humour mixed in to keep it fresh. A few big names – Hella Jongerius, Gijs Bakker and Marcel Wanders – are known internationally, but the best work often comes out of collectives such as Droog and Moooi.

To see Dutch design in action, check out Frozen Fountain (p61) and its tongue-in-cheek versions of Delftware and traditional textiles, as well as patchwork tables made from salvaged wood. At Droog (p136) in Nieuwmarkt, signature designs employ surreal wit, such as a chandelier made of 80-plus light bulbs clustered like fish eggs, or an off-centre umbrella, surely inspired by the country's blustery weather. For bargain designs, all-purpose shop Hema (p41) has developed a cult following by commissioning design students to put a spin on everything from espresso cups to handbags. Once you have a hand towel with a rivet in one corner for hanging, you'll wonder how you lived without it!

Korsakoff

LIVE MUSIC

33 ⭐ Map p48, B6

It's dark. It's a little dirty. And the punk rock chick in the corner is wearing an outfit you haven't seen since Kurt Cobain was alive. Welcome to the heavy metal/punk/industrial heart beat of the Jordaan. There are two levels of dancing, a diverse crowd and a video screen projecting everything from '90s grunge to '70s new wave to techno, depending on the night. (☎625 78 54; www.korsakoffamsterdam.nl; Lijnbaansgracht 161; ⏰from 10pm; 🚊7/10/17 Elandsgracht)

Café Soundgarden

LIVE MUSIC

34 ⭐ Map p48, A6

Somehow Soundgarden's handful of pool tables, 1980s pinball machines, unkempt DJs and lovably surly bar-tenders add up to an ineffable magic. Bands occasionally make an appearance, and the waterfront terrace scene is like an impromptu party in someone's backyard. All walks of life swig here: the common denominator isn't fashion, age or politics – it's a diehard love of rock and roll. (www.cafesoundgarden.nl; Marnixstraat 164-166; 🚊10/13/14/17 Marnixstraat)

Movies

CINEMA

35 ⭐ Map p48, C1

This *gezellig* art deco cinema (the oldest in Amsterdam, dating from 1912) features indie films alongside mainstream flicks, often in English. From Sunday to Thursday you can treat yourself to a meal in the restaurant (a special 'dinner and movie ticket' starts at €22.50) or grab a premovie tipple at its equally inviting cafe-bar. (☎638

60 16; www.themovies.nl; Haarlemmerdijk 161; 🚋3 Haarlemmerplein)

Maloe Melo   BLUES

36 ⭐ Map p48, B7

Maloe Melo is the free-wheeling, fun-loving altar of Amsterdam's tiny blues scene. The dingy but atmospheric venue often adds bluegrass and soul to the calendar, too. (☏420 45 92; www.maloemelo.com; Lijnbaansgracht 163; 🚋7/10/17 Elandsgracht)

De Nieuwe Anita   LIVE MUSIC

37 ⭐ Map p48, A5

A stone's throw west of the Jordaan (across the Singel), De Nieuwe Anita is the neighbourhood clubhouse. It's an intimate living-room-like art lounge that's expanded for noise rockers, with a great cafe onsite. (☏415 35 12; www.denieuweanita.nl; Frederik Hendrikstraat 111; 🚋3 Hugo de Grootplein)

Shopping

Frozen Fountain   DESIGN, HOMEWARES

38 🔒 Map p48, C7

The city's best-known showcase of furniture and interior design crams two canal houses full of the coolest, cleverest gadgets you're likely to come across. The daring wares are offbeat and memorable (designer penknives, kitchen gadgets and that birthday gift for the impossible-to-wow friend), though they don't come cheap.

(www.frozenfountain.nl; Prinsengracht 645; 🚋1/2/5 Prinsengracht)

De Kaaskamer   FOOD & DRINK

39 🔒 Map p48, C7

The name means 'cheese room' and it is indeed stacked to the rafters with Dutch and organic varieties, as well as olives, tapenades, salads and other picnic ingredients. You try before you buy, and if it's too much to take home a mondo wheel of Gouda you can at least procure a cheese and/or meat sandwich or a baguette to take away. (www.kaaskamer.nl; Runstraat 7; ⏱noon-6pm Mon, 9am-6pm Tue-Fri, 9am-5pm Sat, noon-5pm Sun; 🚋1/2/5 Spui)

Rock Archive   ART

40 🔒 Map p48, C4

The whites are white and the blacks are black at this professional shop of limited-edition rock and roll prints. Robert Plant, Debbie Harry, Sting and tons of others are all here to be had for small change, in a format of your choice. (☏423 04 89; www.rockarchive.com; Prinsengracht 110; ⏱2-6pm Wed-Fri, noon-6pm Sat & by appointment; 🚋13/14/17 Westermarkt)

Boekie Woekie   BOOKS

41 🔒 Map p48, C6

While other shops handle art books, this artist-run bookstore sells books as art, created by artists specifically for this medium. Some tell stories (elegantly illustrated, naturally), others are riffs on graphic motifs. The stock, including handmade paper and cards, will keep you browsing for a long time. (Berenstraat 16; ⏰noon-6pm; 🚋13/14/17 Westermarkt)

Het Oud-Hollandsch Snoepwinkeltje
FOOD & DRINK

42 🔒 Map p48, C4

This corner shop is lined with jar after apothecary jar of Dutch penny sweets with flavours from chocolate to coffee, all manner of fruit and the salty Dutch liquorice known as *zoute drop*. (📞420 73 90; www.snoepwinkeltje.com; Egelantiersdwarsstraat 2; ⏰Tue-Sun; 🚋3/10 Marnixplein)

Understand
Drop the Liquorice

The Dutch love their lollies, the most famous of which is *drop*, the word for all varieties of liquorice. It may be gummy-soft or tough as leather, shaped like coins or miniature cars, but the most important distinction is between *zoete* (sweet) and *zoute* (salty, also called *salmiak*). The latter is often an alarming surprise, even for avowed fans of the black stuff. But with such a range of textures and additional flavours – mint, honey, laurel – even liquorice sceptics might be converted. Het Oud-Hollandsch Snoepwinkeltje is a good place to do a taste test.

Kitsch Kitchen
HOUSEWARES

43 🔒 Map p48, C5

You want it flowered, frilly, colourful, over the top or just made from plastic? The chances are you'll find it here – Kitsch Kitchen has handbags, homewares, toys, doll gowns, lamps, Mexican tableclothes, pink plastic chandeliers from India and, of course, bouquets of plastic flowers. (📞622 82 61; www.kitschkitchen.nl; Rozengracht 8-12; 🚋13/14/17 Westermarkt)

Lady Day
CLOTHING

44 🔒 Map p48, D6

This is the premier location for unearthing spotless vintage clothes from Holland and elsewhere. The leather jackets, swingin' 1960s and '70s wear, and woollen sailors' coats are well-priced winners. Some men's suits and new shoes also peek out among the wares. (www.ladydayvintage.com; Hartenstraat 9; 🚋13/14/17 Westermarkt)

Marlies Dekkers
LINGERIE

45 🔒 Map p48, C6

The preeminent Dutch lingerie designer Marlies Dekkers is known for her subtle hints at bondage, detailed on exquisite undergarments. Summer sees an equally enticing range of swimwear. The shop itself is a sultry bastion of decadence, with handpainted wallpaper and a titillating lounge area with a fireplace. (www.marliesdekkers.com; Berenstraat 18; 🚋13/14/17 Westermarkt)

De Kaaskamer (p61)

Scotch & Soda
CLOTHING

46 Map p48, D7

For a high-style shopping spree, head here first. Couples can compare sleek outfits as both men's and women's fashion lines fill the racks. The chic outerwear is especially smart – guaranteed to keep you looking impossibly cool even during the most tempestuous Dutch weather. Other branches of the store are scattered around the area, too. (www.scotch-soda.com; Huidenstraat 5; ☉Mon-Sat; ☐1/2/5 Spui)

Unlimited Delicious
FOOD & DRINK

47 Map p48, D2

Is it ever! It's tempting to dive into the sculptural cakes and tarts, but – if you can – walk past them to the dozens of varieties of chocolates made in-house. Some of the more outlandish combinations (that somehow work) are rosemary sea salt, caramel cayenne and citron *witbier* (white beer). Also on offer are tastings, and bonbon and patisserie workshops. (www.unlimited delicious.nl; Haarlemmerstraat 122; ☉9am-6pm Mon-Sat, ☐1/2/5/13/17 Martelaarsgracht)

Local Life
Exploring Westerpark & Western Islands

Getting There

The area borders the Jordaan to the north-west; it's 1.6km from Centraal Station.

🚊 Trams 3 and 10 swing by the area.

🚌 Bus 22 goes to Het Schip.

A reedy wilderness, a post-industrial culture complex and a drawbridge-filled adventure await those who make the trip to Westerpark and the Western Islands. It's a whole different world, a stone's throw from Centraal Station. Architectural and foodie hot spots add to the hip, eco-urban mashup. The area's rags-to-riches story is proto-typical Amsterdam: abandoned factoryland hits the skids, squatters salvage it, and it rises again in creative fashion.

1 Amsterdam School Architecture

The remarkable housing project **Het Schip** (📞418 28 85; www.hetschip.nl; Spaarndammerplantsoen 140; admission €7.50; ⏱11am-5pm Tue-Sun; 🚋22 Zaanstraat) is the pinnacle of Amsterdam School architecture. Michel de Klerk designed the triangular block, loosely resembling a ship, for railway employees. It now hosts a small museum.

2 Patch of Green

From Het Schip, walk southeast along the train tracks and cut through a small underpass to **Westerpark** (Haarlemmerweg; 🚋3 Haarlemmerplein). The pond-dappled green space is a cool-cat hang-out that blends into **Westergasfabriek**, a former gasworks transformed into an edgy cultural park.

3 Terrace Drinks

On sunny afternoons young, artsy professionals flock to the massive outdoor terrace (and one coveted comfy swing) at **Westergasterras** (www.westergasterras.nl; Klönneplein 4; ⏱from 11am Mon-Fri, from 10am Sat & Sun; 🚋10 Van Limburg-Stirumstraat). A toasty fireplace makes the cafe equally inviting indoors. It's perfect for a vino and mackerel salad sandwich. Late at night it morphs into a club.

4 Caribbean Flavour

Toko MC (📞475 04 25; www.tokomc.nl; Polonceaukade 5; mains €17-20; ⏱from noon Tue-Sun; 🚋10 Van Limburg-Stirumstraat) fulfils many needs. It's part Caribbean-soulfood restaurant (think grilled sardines and baked pumpkin), part paper-lantern-lit bar pouring cane-sugar cocktails, and part late-night club where DJs spin world music. The attached MC Theatre hosts multicultural music and dance performances.

5 Western Islands

The **Western Islands** (Westelijke Eilanden; 🚋3 Zoutkeetsgracht) were originally home to shipworks and the West India Trading Company's warehouses, which buzzed with activity in the early 1600s. The district is a world unto itself, cut through with canals and linked with small drawbridges. It's well worth a wander among the charming homes and artists' studios.

6 Scenic Zandhoek

Be sure to visit the **Zandhoek** (Realeneiland; 🚋3 Zoutkeetsgracht), a photogenic stretch of waterfront on the eastern shore. Now a modern yacht harbour (with motorboat rentals available), back in the 17th century it was a 'sandmarket', where ships would purchase bags of the stuff for ballast.

7 Foodie Love at Marius

Foodies swoon over pocket-sized **Marius** (📞422 78 80; Barentszstraat 173; mains €26-38, set menu €47.50; ⏱dinner Tue-Sat; 🚋3 Zoutkeetsgracht). Chef Kees, an alumnus of California's Chez Panisse, shops daily at local markets, then creates his menu from what he finds (eg grilled prawns with fava bean purée). He also operates a sausage-and-wine bar a few doors west.

Explore

Southern Canal Belt

Two clubby nightlife districts anchor the Southern Canal Belt: Leidseplein and Rembrandtplein. Both are neon-lit, one-stop shops for partygoers. In between lie several intriguing museums – including the art blockbuster Hermitage Amsterdam – and restaurants, cafes and shops galore. During the Golden Age the city's wealthiest residents lived in the 'hood, so add in mansions set on gorgeous canals to the mix, too.

KIMBERLEY COOLE / GETTY IMAGES ©

The Sights in a Day

☀ Devote the morning to whatever mega art exhibit the **Hermitage Amsterdam** (p72) is showing. Then stroll over to the **Tassenmuseum Hendrikje** (p73), a museum dedicated to handbags and purses throughout history – heaven for 'ladies who lunch'!

☀ Begin the afternoon at Rembrandtplein and do the tourist thing. Snap a photo with the master painter's statue, eat a *kroket* (croquette) at **Van Dobben** (p74), and pick up souvenirs at the **Ajax Experience** (p81) or **Heineken City Store** (p81). Finish with a drink at **De Kroon** (p76). Next saunter over to **Museum Van Loon** (p72) for a look at the moneyed canal-house lifestyle, and to **FOAM** (p72) for renowned photography exhibits.

☾ For dinner, choose among the smart restaurants along Utrechtsestraat – maybe **Tempo Doeloe** (p75) or **Segugio** (p75). You'll need a solid meal to energise the evening's activities around Leidseplein. See what's on at **Paradiso** (p79), **Melkweg** (p79), **Boom Chicago** (p80) and **Jazz Café Alto** (p79). Prefer something more laid back? Try beery **Café de Spuyt** (p77) or **Eijlders** (p76).

For a local's day in the Southern Canal Belt, see p68.

○ Local Life

Strolling the Southern Canal Belt (p68)

♥ Best of Amsterdam

Museums & Galleries
Hermitage Amsterdam (p72)

FOAM (p72)

Museum Van Loon (p72)

Tassenmuseum Hendrikje (p73)

Entertainment
Paradiso (p79)

Melkweg (p79)

Jazz Café Alto (p79)

Eating
Van Dobben (p74)

Tempo Doeloe (p75)

Drinking
De Kroon (p76)

Bo Cinq (p76)

Café de Spuyt (p77)

Getting There

🚊 **Tram** Trams 1, 2, 5, 7 and 10 go to Leidseplein. To Rembrandtplein, take tram 4, which travels down Utrechtsestraat (full of restaurants). Trams 16, 24 and 25 cut through the centre of the neighbourhood down busy Vijzelstraat.

Local Life
Strolling the Southern Canal Belt

Puttin' on the ritz is nothing new to the Southern Canal Belt. Most of the area was built at the end of the 17th century, when Amsterdam was wallowing in Golden Age cash. A wander through reveals grand mansions, swanky antique shops, indulgent patisseries and a one-of-a-kind kitty museum. And while it's all stately it's certainly not snobby.

1 Flower Market

The canalside **Bloemenmarkt** (Singel, btwn Muntplein & Koningsplein; admission free; ⊙9am-5.30pm Mon-Sat, 11am-5.30pm Sun; 🚋1/2/5 Koningsplein) has been here since the 1860s, when gardeners used to sail up the Amstel and sell from their boats. Exotic bulbs are the main stock, though cut flowers brighten the stalls, too. Buy a bouquet: there's no better way to feel like a local than walking around with flowers in the crook of your arm.

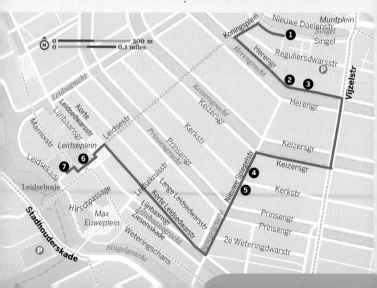

❷ Golden Bend Riches

During the Golden Age, the **Golden Bend** (Gouden Bocht; Herengracht, btwn Leidsestraat & Vijzelstraat) was the 'it' spot, where the wealthiest Amsterdammers lived, loved and ruled their affairs. Look up at the mansions as you walk along the Herengracht. Many date from the 1660s, and thanks to some lobbying at city hall, the gables here were allowed to be twice as wide as the standard Amsterdam model.

❸ Odd Art at the Kattenkabinet

The only Golden Bend abode that's open to the public is the **Kattenkabinet** (Cats Cabinet; ☎626 53 78; www .kattenkabinet.nl; Herengracht 497; adult/ child €6/3; ☉10am-4pm Mon-Fri, noon-5pm Sat & Sun; 🚊4/16/24/25 Keizersgracht), an offbeat museum devoted to cat-related art. A Picasso drawing, kitschy kitty lithographs and odd pieces of ephemera like a cat pinball machine cram the creaky old house. A few happy live felines lounge around on the window seats.

❹ Spiegel Quarter Antiques

When it's time to decorate that mansion, folks head to the long line of shops along Nieuwe Spiegelstraat and Spiegelgracht, aka the **Spiegel Quarter**. The perfect Delft vase or 16th-century wall map will most assuredly be hiding among the antique stores, bric-a-brac shops and commercial art galleries.

❺ Chocolate at Pâtisserie Pompadour

The society ladies know where to replenish after shopping: mod, chichi **Pâtisserie Pompadour** (www.patisserie pompadour.com; Kerkstraat 148; ☉10am-6pm Tue-Fri, 9am-5.30pm Sat; 🚊16/24/25 Keizersgracht). Join them in nibbling on Belgian-style chocolates and pastries. The pièce de résistance is the hot chocolate, a scoop of dark sweetness melted by piping, creamy milk.

❻ Theatre Time

The neo-Renaissance **Stadsschouwburg** (City Theatre; ☎624 23 11; www .stadsschouwburgamsterdam.nl; Leidseplein 26; ☉box office noon-6pm Mon-Sat; 🚊1/2/5/7/10 Leidseplein) takes pride of place on the Leidseplein. The regal venue, built in 1894, is used for large-scale plays, operettas and the Holland Festival, the country's biggest arts extravaganza. Amsterdam's main ticket desk is also stashed inside, where you can see what's on and get half-price seats for shows around town.

❼ Drinks at Café Americain

Pull up a chair, order a cappuccino and watch the world spin by at **Café Americain** (Eden Amsterdam American Hotel, Leidsekade 97; ☉from 7am; 🚊1/2/5/7/10 Leidseplein). The art deco monument, opened in 1902, has huge stained-glass windows overlooking Leidseplein, a lovely, library-like reading table and a great terrace. It serves a sandwich-and-macaron-stacked high tea daily at 2pm.

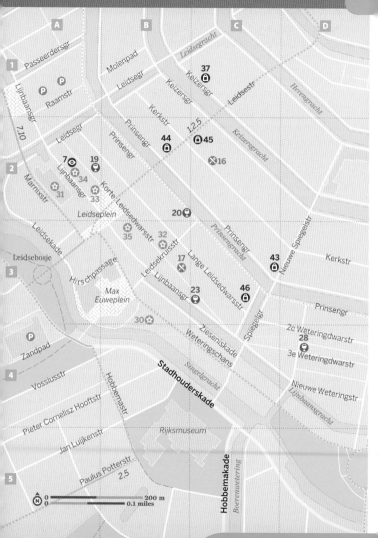

Sights

Hermitage Amsterdam   MUSEUM

1 ⊙ Map p70, H2

Given Peter the Great's admiration for Golden Age Amsterdam, this satellite of St Petersburg's State Hermitage Museum makes perfect sense. It occupies the vast Amstelhof, an alms house since the 17th century. Prestigious exhibits, such as treasures from the Russian palace or masterworks by Van Gogh and Gaugin, change about twice per year, and they're as blockbuster as you'd expect. (☑530 74 88; www .hermitage.nl; Amstel 51; adult/child €15/free; ☉10am-5pm; ⊠9/14 Waterlooplein)

FOAM   MUSEUM

2 ⊙ Map p70, E2

Simple, functional but roomy galleries, some with skylights or grand windows for natural light, make this museum an excellent space for all genres of photography. Two storeys of exhibition space create a great setting for admiring the changing exhibits from photographers of world renown, including Sir Cecil Beaton, Annie Leibovitz and Henri Cartier-Bresson. (Fotografie Museum Amsterdam; www.foam .nl; Keizersgracht 609; adult/child €8.50/ free; ☉10am-6pm Sat-Wed, to 9pm Thu & Fri; ⊠16/24/25 Keizersgracht)

Museum Van Loon   MUSEUM

3 ⊙ Map p70, E3

Arguably the best of the canal-house museums, this 1672 mansion was first home to painter Ferdinand Bol. In the 19th century the Van Loon family (descendants of Willem van Loon, cofounder of the Dutch East India Company) moved in, and they still occupy the upper floors. Take your time wandering through the shadowy rooms adorned with rich wallpaper, worn carpets and well-used Louis XV furniture. (☑624 52 55; www.museum vanloon.nl; Keizersgracht 672; adult/child €8/4; ☉11am-5pm Wed-Mon; ⊠16/24/25 Keizersgracht)

Stadsarchief   HISTORICAL ARCHIVE

4 ⊙ Map p70, E2

The Amsterdam archives occupy a monumental bank building that dates from 1923. When you step inside, head to the left to the enormous tiled basement vault and displays of archive gems such as the 1942 police report on Anne Frank's bike theft. Well-done temporary exhibits fill the gallery space upstairs; sometimes these have an entry fee (up to €6). (Municipal Archives; ☑251 15 11; www.stadsarchief .amsterdam.nl; Vijzelstraat 32; admission free; ☉10am-5pm Tue-Fri, noon-5pm Sat & Sun)

Museum Willet-Holthuysen   MUSEUM

5 ⊙ Map p70, G2

This mansion has been a museum since 1895, when a wealthy widow gave the city her home and her husband's assorted treasures – furniture, paintings and loads of 18th-century china. It's a bit fussier than nearby

Museum Van Loon, but the objects are lovely. The 3rd-floor 'collection room' impresses with its stained glass and red velvet wallpaper. Don't miss the rococo, 18th-century garden out the back. (☑523 18 22; www.willetholthuysen. nl; Herengracht 605; adult/child €8/free; ⊙10am-5pm Mon-Fri, 11am-5pm Sat & Sun; ☒4/9/14 Rembrandtplein)

Tassenmuseum
Hendrikje   MUSEUM

6 ◉ Map p70, F2

Dedicated entirely to handbags, this chic canal-house museum is surprisingly interesting even for nonfashionistas. You'll find everything from a crumpled 16th-century goatskin pouch to dainty art deco and design classics by Chanel, Gucci and Versace. Even if you don't see the '80s touch-tone phone bag, the 17th-century interiors (and the tearoom's delicious cake aromas) are worth the entrance price. (Museum of Bags & Purses; ☑524 64 52; www.tassen museum.nl; Herengracht 573; adult/child €8.50/free; ⊙10am-5pm; ☒4/9/14 Rembrandtplein)

Greenbox Museum   MUSEUM

7 ◉ Map p70, A2

Obsessive Amsterdam at its best: at this fascinating collection of contemporary art from Saudi Arabia, you get a personal tour from the enthusiastic owner himself. (☑062 428 28 84; www .greenboxmuseum.com; Korte Leidsedwarsstraat 12; admission €5; ⊙1-5pm Wed-Fri; ☒1/2/5/7/10 Leidseplein)

Museum Van Loon

Eating

Piet de Leeuw   STEAKHOUSE €€

8 ✖ Map p70, E4

Situated in a building that dates from 1900, this place has been a steakhouse and hang-out since the 1940s, and the dark and cosy atmosphere has barely changed since then. If you don't manage to get your own table, you may meet folks from all over at a common table, eating well-priced steaks with toppings such as onions, mushrooms or bacon, served with salad and piping-hot *frites* (fries). (☑623 71 81; www.pietdeleeuw.nl; Noorderstraat 11; mains €13-20; ⊙lunch Mon-Fri, dinner nightly; ☒16/24/25 Prinsengracht)

Van Dobben

SANDWICH SHOP €

9 Map p70, F1

Open since the 1940s, the venerable Van Dobben has white-tile walls and white-coated counter men who specialise in snappy banter. Traditional meaty Dutch fare is its forte: try the *pekelvlees* (something close to corned beef), or make it a *halfom* (if you're keen on that being mixed with liver). The *kroketten* are the best in town and compulsory after a late-night Rembrandtplein booze-up. (☎624 42 00; www.eetsalonvandobben.nl; Korte Reguliersdwarsstraat 5; items €2.75-6.50; ⏰10am-9pm Mon-Thu, to 2am Fri & Sat, 11.30am-9pm Sun; ☐4/9/14 Rembrandtplein)

Local Life
Reguliersgracht

It's easy to focus on the raucous nightlife and forget that one of Amsterdam's most romantic canals flows in the neighbourhood. The **Reguliersgracht**, aka the canal of seven bridges, is especially idyllic in the evening when its humpbacked arches glow with tiny white lights. To get the money shot, stand with your back to the Thorbeckeplein and the Herengracht flowing directly in front of you to the left and right. Lean over the bridge and look straight ahead down the Reguliersgracht. Ahhh. Now kiss your sweetie.

Loekie

SANDWICH SHOP €

10 Map p70, G2

This delicatessen piles fresh, delicious ingredients into its takeaway sandwiches, such as smoked beef with egg and salt, or warm goat's cheese with pine nuts and honey. Ask for the English menu if it's not on the counter already. (www.loekie.net; Utrechtsestraat 57; sandwiches €5-9; ⏰9am-6pm Mon-Sat, to 1pm Wed; ☐4 Keizersgracht)

Ponte Arcari

ITALIAN €€

11 Map p70, F2

When you can't jet off to Venice for the weekend, Ponte Arcari will have to suffice. Sink your fork into nightly dinner specials like eggplant rollatini au gratin, and you'll find yourself still sighing over it days later. While there are many intimate, canalside restaurants, few are this cosy. It's a stone's throw from Rembrandtplein and yet a world away. (☎625 08 53; Herengracht 534; mains €12-28; ⏰lunch Tue-Sat, dinner nightly; ☐4/9/14 Rembrandtplein)

Le Zinc...et les Autres

FRENCH €€

12 Map p70, F3

This cosy old canal-house restaurant is an unapologetically old-fashioned affair, with candlelight, wine and romance to spare. The menu matches the vibe, with rustic dishes like pigeon and rabbit, and an option of matched reds and whites alongside each course. Vegetarians can fill up, too – maybe a dish with beetroot and goat's cheese or an oven-roasted tomato tart. (📞622 90 44; www.lezinc.nl; Prinsengracht 999; mains €15-30, 3-course menu €34.50; ⏱5.30-11pm Mon-Sat; ♿; 🚊4 Prinsengracht)

Tempo Doeloe INDONESIAN €€€

13 ❌ Map p70, G3

Tempo Doeloe is one of Amsterdam's most respected (and hottest-spiced!) Indonesian restaurants. It's a slightly formal place that gives solo diners a chance to try the sampler-plate *rijst-tafel* (many places will do it only for a minimum of two people). But the à la carte options are arguably better. Reservations are required – or visit the owners' more casual Tujuh Maret next door. (📞625 67 18; www.tempodoeloe restaurant.nl; Utrechtsestraat 75; mains €20-25, rijsttafel & set menus €28-40; ⏱dinner Mon-Sat; ♿; 🚊4 Keizersgracht)

Segugio ITALIAN €€€

14 ❌ Map p70, G3

This fashionably minimalist storefront with two levels of seating is the sort of place other chefs go for a good dinner. It's known for risotto and high-quality ingredients combined with a sure hand. Book ahead – it's almost always busy. (📞330 15 03; www.segugio.nl; Utrecht-sestraat 96; pastas €17-20, mains €24-36; ⏱from 6pm Mon-Sat; 🚊; 4 Prinsengracht)

Bouchon du Centre FRENCH €€

15 ❌ Map p70, G4

A secret of meat fanatics and Francophiles in the know, this little restaurant isn't for everyone – and it doesn't want to be. There's a changing, daily menu of a few dishes only: bet on it being French, meat-oriented and divine. (📞616 74 14; www.bouchonducentre amsterdam.com; Falckstraat 3; mains from €15; ⏱noon-3pm, 5pm-8pm Wed-Sat; 🚊4 Frederiksplein)

Los Pilones MEXICAN €€

16 ❌ Map p70, C2

Owners Hector and Pedro consistently set the standard among Amsterdam's handful of Mexican restaurants. If you're looking for grilled *bistek* (beef-steak), crispy chicken rolls and fruity mango margaritas in a colourful, social environment, you're definitely in the right place. A few shots from the 60-plus tequila list, and you'll be feeling brave enough to ask for the extra-hot salsa. (www.lospilones.com; Kerkstraat 63; mains €13-20; ⏱4-10.30pm Tue-Sun; 🚊1/2/5 Prinsengracht)

Taste of Culture CHINESE €€

17 ❌ Map p70, B3

Most restaurants near the Leidseplein dish up greasy stuff for tourists and late-night drinkers, but this one bucks the trend, with freshly prepared regional dishes enjoyed by a big Chinese clientele. Good options are the razor clams and various stir-fried greens. Added bonus: the kitchen is open till midnight, and later on weekends. (📞427 11 36; www.tasteofculture.net; Korte Leidsedwarsstraat 139-141; mains €15-23;

⊘5pm-1am Sun-Thu, 5pm-3am Fri & Sat;
🚋1/2/5/7/10 Leidseplein)

Drinking

De Kroon
GRAND CAFE

18 🚋 Map p70, G1

A popular venue for media events and
movie-premiere parties that's been restored to its original 1898 splendour:
expect high ceilings, velvet chairs and
the chance to wave at the hoi polloi
below on Rembrandtplein from your
second-storey windowside perch. Or
sit at the English-library-themed bar
and be mesmerised by the curious

display of 19th-century medical and
scientific equipment. (www.dekroon.nl;
Rembrandtplein 17-1; ⊘from 11am; 🚋4/9/14
Rembrandtplein)

Eijlders
BROWN CAFE

19 🚋 Map p70, A2

During WWII Eijlders was a meeting
place for artists who refused to toe
the cultural line imposed by the Nazis,
and the spirit lingers on. It's still an
artists cafe with classical music jams
on the second Sunday of every month,
poetry readings the third Sunday and
lots of locals drinking beer the rest of
the month. (www.eijlders.nl; Korte Leidsedwarsstraat 47; ⊘from noon Fri-Mon, from
4.30pm Tue-Thu; 🚋1/2/5/7/10 Leidseplein)

Bo Cinq
DESIGNER BAR

20 🚋 Map p70, B2

Beautiful people and their admirers
flock to this ultralong, gleaming bar
after work and on into the wee hours.
We dig that on any given night there's
a healthy balance of expats and Dutch
locals. Grab a mojito and strike your
best languid pose on one of the couches as you try to decipher the multiple
languages being spoken around you.
(www.bo5.nl; Prinsengracht 494; ⊘from 5pm
Mon-Sat; 🚋1/2/5 Prinsengracht)

Café Schiller
THEATRE CAFE

21 🚋 Map p70, F2

With a fabulous art deco interior,
this is the sole piece of old-fashioned
charm on the raucous Rembrandt-

🅠 Local Life

Fast Food Favourites

Plucking a deep-fried snack from
the yellow automat windows at
FEBO (📞620 86 15; Leidsestraat 94;
mains €3-6; ⊘11am-3am Sun-Thu, 11am-
4am Fri & Sat; 🚋1/2/5 Prinsengracht) is
a drunken Dutch tradition. We don't
exactly recommend the fare, but
it's there when you need it – especially in the wee hours.

Vegetarian felafel is perfected at
Maoz (📞420 74 35; www.maozusa
.com; Muntplein 1; mains €4-8; ⊘11am-
1am Sun-Thu, to 3am Fri & Sat; 🖊;
🚋4/9/14/24/25 Muntplein). For
around €5 you get four fried chick-
pea balls with pita and unlimited
access to a massive salad bar.
Both FEBO and Maoz have outlets
throughout town.

De Kroon

plein. Walls are lined with portraits of Dutch actors and cabaret artists from the 1920s and '30s. Bar stools and booths are often occupied by tippling journalists and artists, and folks tucking into pre- and post-theatre menus in the back restaurant. (www.cafe schiller.nl; Rembrandtplein 26; ⊘from 4pm Mon-Fri, from 2pm Sat & Sun; 🚊4/9/14 Rembrandtplein)

De Huyschkaemer   DESIGNER BAR

22 🚇 Map p70, G4

With conversation-piece art – like a giant photo of a nude Dutch football team – there's always buzzing chatter at De Huyschkaemer. Nursing a beer next to the big windows on Utrechtsestraat is tempting, but the real action spills out on the street, where a mixed crowd – gay and straight, expat and local, old and young – shakes off the workday. (www.huyschkaemer.nl; Utrechtsestraat 137; 🚊4 Prinsengracht)

Café de Spuyt   BEER CAFE

23 🚇 Map p70, C3

Steps away from the bustling Leidseplein, the bar staff at this mellow, friendly cafe will happily guide you through the massive chalkboard menu of more than 100 beers, from Belgian Trappist ales to American Sierra Nevada. (www.cafedespuyt.nl; Korte Leidsedwarsstraat 86; ⊘from 4pm; 🚊1/2/5/7/10 Leidseplein)

Understand

How to Eat a Herring

‘Hollandse Nieuwe’ isn’t a fashion trend – it’s the fresh catch of super-tasty herring, raked in every June. The Dutch love it, and you’ll see vendors selling the salty fish all over town. Although Dutch tradition calls for dangling the herring above your mouth, this isn’t the way it’s done in Amsterdam. Here the fish is served chopped in chunks and eaten with a toothpick, topped with *eitjes* (chopped onions) and *zuur* (sweet pickles). A *broodje haring* (herring roll) is even handier, as the fluffy white roll holds on the toppings and keeps your fingers fish-fat-free – think of it as an edible napkin.

Air
CLUB

24 Map p70, G1

One of Amsterdam’s ‘it’ clubs, Air has an environmentally friendly design and a unique tiered dance floor. Nice touches include free mini lockers and refillable drink cards that preclude fussing with change at the bar. Though the place gets packed, it has ultrahigh ceilings and it feels like there’s still plenty of room to get funky. Cover charges average between €9 and €15. (820 06 70; www.air.nl; Amstelstraat 16; Thu-Sun; 4/9/14 Rembrandtplein)

Door 74
COCKTAIL BAR

25 Map p70, E1

The drinks poured in here are far and away Amsterdam’s best cocktails, served in an elegant but unpretentious atmosphere, behind an unmarked door. Mixologists shake up concoctions like the Peanut Butter and Jelly (bourbon and raspberry syrup)

and Hopscotch to Holland (*jenever*, citrus and herbs). For entry, you must call or send a text message to reserve seats. (063 404 51 22; www.door-74.nl; Reguliersdwarsstraat 74; from 8pm; 9/14 Rembrandtplein)

Studio 80
CLUB

26 Map p70, F1

It’s all about the (electronic) music at this raw space, which functions as much as a studio and radio station as a club. Bespectacled hipsters, glittering fashionistas and androgynous arty types mix it up on the dimly lit dance floor. Cheapish entry (usually between €6 to €16) guarantees a young crowd. (521 83 33; www.studio-80.nl; Rembrandtplein 17; Wed-Sat; 4/9/14 Rembrandtplein)

Café Langereis
CAFE

27 Map p70, H1

A lovely cafe along the Amstel river near Rembrandtplein, Café Langereis feels like it has been around forever.

That's because the young owner scoured the city for antique fixtures and furniture to re-create the lived-in feel of the vintage brown cafes she had long admired. Freshly ground coffee, fresh flowers on the tables and a classic rock soundtrack add to the vibe. (www.cafelangereis.com; Amstel 202; ⏰from 11am; 🚊4/9/14 Rembrandtplein)

Café de Wetering   BROWN CAFE

28 ☕ Map p70, D4

Bursting with Amsterdammers of all ages, local secret Café de Wetering is easy to miss. Tucked in an off-the-beaten-path street, it's not far from the famed antiques corridor of Nieuwe Spiegelstraat. Perch on the upper level by the fireplace, or sit at the bar to chat with the wisecracking bartenders. On chilly days, it's an ideal refuge. (Weteringstraat 37; 🚊7/10 Spiegelgracht)

De Koffie Salon   CAFE

29 ☕ Map p70, G4

The airy, sophisticated vibe here is genuine, not a put-on affair, with communal tables that invite conversation, magazine sharing, and gazing at that cute stranger who's lost in a novel. Friendly baristas whip up badass strong espresso that goes perfectly with the *stroopwafels* (thin waffles filled with syrup) and other bakery goodies. The cafe has branches in De Pijp and Vondelpark. (www.dekoffiesalon.nl; Utrechtsestraat 130; 🚊4 Prinsengracht)

Entertainment

Paradiso   LIVE MUSIC, CLUB

30 ⭐ Map p70, B3

Worship rock and roll in a gorgeous old church. Artists from The Roots to Lady Gaga rock the Main Hall while you wonder if the stained-glass windows just might shatter. Midweek club nights with low cover charges lure the young and the restless, while the Small Hall upstairs provides an intimate venue to see up-and-coming bands from around the world. (www.paradiso.nl; Weteringschans 6; 🚊7/10 Spiegelgracht)

Melkweg   LIVE MUSIC, CLUB

31 ⭐ Map p70, A2

The 'Milky Way' – it's housed in a former dairy – is a dazzling galaxy of diverse music. One night it's reggae or punk, the next night heavy metal lures in the leather-jacketed biker crowd. Dance nights might spin electronica in one room and '90s rock in the other. Check the website for cutting-edge cinema and theatre offerings, too. (www.melkweg.nl; Lijnbaansgracht 234a; 🚊1/2/5/7/10 Leidseplein)

Jazz Café Alto   JAZZ

32 ⭐ Map p70, B3

Smack in Amsterdam's touristy heart is this renowned gem of a jazz club. It's so small that you feel as though you're part of the musical conversation between the band members.

Tuesdays mean salsa and Latin jazz. Doors open at 9pm but music starts around 10pm – get there early if you want to snag a seat. (www.jazz-cafe-alto .nl; Korte Leidsedwarsstraat 115; ⊙from 9pm; 🚃1/2/5/7/10 Leidseplein)

Boom Chicago & Chicago Social Club   COMEDY, CLUB

33 ⭐ Map p70, A2

In 2011 Boom Chicago branched out to become a trinity of Leidseplein entertainment: it's a comedy club, a late-night bar and a nightclub. The hilarious English-language improv troupe – Boom's mainstay – has been playing to enthusiastic crowds since 1993. The topical shows riff on local and European issues and are a surprisingly good place to get the pulse of Amsterdam politics. (📞423 01 01;

☑ Top Tip
Get Uit & About

Not sure how to spend your evening? Head to the Last Minute Ticket Shop desk at the **Uitburo** (📞621 13 11; www.amsterdamsuitburo .nl; Leidseplein 26; ⊙10am-7pm Mon-Fri, 10am-6pm Sat, noon-6pm Sun; 🚃1/2/5/7/10 Leidseplein), in the corner of the Stadsschouwburg on the Leidseplein. Comedy, dance, concerts, even club nights are often available at a significant discount – and handily marked 'LNP' (language no problem) if understanding Dutch isn't vital.

---

www.boomchicago.nl; Leidseplein 12; ⊙box office 2-8.30pm Mon-Wed, from 1pm Thu-Sun; 🚃1/2/5/7/10 Leidseplein)

Sugar Factory   LIVE MUSIC, CLUB

34 ⭐ Map p70, A2

The vibe at this self-described 'cutting-edge multidisciplinary night theatre' is always welcoming and creative. It's definitely not your average club – most nights start with music, cinema, or a dance or spoken-word performance, followed by late-night DJs and dancing. Sunday's Wicked Jazz Sounds party is a sweet one, bringing DJs, musicians, singers and actors together to improvise. (www.sugarfactory.nl; Lijnbaansgracht 238; 🚃1/2/5/7/10 Leidseplein)

Up   LIVE MUSIC, CLUB

35 ⭐ Map p70, B3

Private arts society De Kring sponsors this small, quirky club, where you could encounter DJs, live bands, performance art – all for a young, eclectic crowd. The sound system rocks. Occasionally entrance is through De Kring, at Kleine Gartmanplantsoen 7-9; check the website. (📞623 69 85; www.clubup.nl; Korte Leidsedwarsstraat 26; admission €6-10; ⊙Thu-Sun; 🚃1/2/5/7/10 Leidseplein)

Pathé Tuschinskitheater   CINEMA

36 ⭐ Map p70, F1

Extensively refurbished, Amsterdam's most famous cinema is worth visiting for its sumptuous art deco/Amsterdam School interior. It features a huge handmade carpet and a striking cupola that should never meet the gaze of someone on hallucinogens. The *grote zaal* (main auditorium) generally screens blockbusters; the smaller theatres play art-house and indie films. (www.pathe.nl/tuschinski; Reguliersbreestraat 26-34; 🚊4/9/14 Rembrandtplein)

Shopping
Young Designers United CLOTHING
37 🅐 Map p70, C1

Angelika Groenendijk Wasylewski's boutique is a showcase for young designers (mainly Dutch). It regularly rotates the racks but on our visit we spotted Monique Poolman's strong, designed cuts; Letke de Roos' fun, feminine pieces; Heidi Long's striking collection; and Susa Plaza's sporty, comfortable look. (www.ydu.nl; Keizersgracht 447; ⏱Mon-Sat; 🚊1/2/5 Keizersgracht)

Kaas Huis Tromp FOOD & DRINK
38 🅐 Map p70, G3

Perhaps a more fitting name for this 'cheese house' would be a temple, for it's a wonderful place to come if you want to worship fermented dairy products from all over Holland and the world. Fortunately, Henk, the affable proprietor, knows that this is best done with plenty of free samples – a concept that most other cheese shops in Amsterdam miss. (www.kaashuistromp.nl; Utrechtsestraat 90; 🚊4 Prinsengracht)

Heineken City Store SOUVENIRS
39 🅐 Map p70, H1

Heineken's multistorey concept store glows cool and green, just like a frosty bottle of the brew itself. Some of the logoed gear is over the top (the chic jackets), but the decorated beer bottles in the huge fridge make groovy souvenirs. We especially like the primary-colour block-print ones à la Dutch artist Piet Mondrian. This store carries more wares than the brewery's shop in De Pijp. (Amstelstraat 31; ⏱11am-8pm Mon-Sat; 🚊4/9/14 Rembrandtplein)

Ajax Experience Store SOUVENIRS
40 🅐 Map p70, G1

Amsterdam's beloved football club recently opened a museum devoted to the team (very interactive, very youth-oriented, very costly: for true fans only). What you want is the store inside, which stocks red-and-white team-logoed hats, shirts and whatnot – vintage local souvenirs. (www.ajaxexperienceamsterdam.com; Utrechtsestraat 9; ⏱11am-7pm; 🚊4/9/14 Rembrandtplein)

Concerto MUSIC
41 🅐 Map p70, G3

Most excellent. This rambling shop, which spreads itself over several buildings, has Amsterdam's best selection of new and secondhand CDs and records; you could easily spend hours on end browsing in here. It's often cheap and always interesting, and has good listening facilities so you can try

Window display, Eduard Kramer

before you buy. (Utrechtsestraat 52-60; 🚋4 Keizersgracht)

Stadsboekwinkel BOOKS

42 🅐 Map p70, E2

Run by the city printer, this is the best source for books about Amsterdam's history, urban development, ecology and politics. Most titles are in Dutch (you can always look at the pictures), but you'll also find some in English. It's in the Stadsarchief (Municipal Archives) building. (www.stadsboekwinkel.nl; Vijzelstraat 32; ☺Tue-Sun; 🚋16/24/25 Keizersgracht)

Eduard Kramer ANTIQUES

43 🅐 Map p70, C3

Specialising in antique Dutch wall and floor tiles, Eduard Kramer has an extensive tile collection that sits alongside books, jewellery and vintage homewares including glassware and Delft pottery. Stroll a few doors down to browse the expanded selection of art and tiles at the new addition at Prinsengracht 807, a gorgeously refurbished old grocery store. (www.antique-tileshop.nl; Nieuwe Spiegelstraat 64; ☺Tue-Sun; 🚋16/24/25 Keizersgracht)

Cora Kemperman
CLOTHING

44 Map p70, B2

Kemperman was once a designer with large Dutch fashion houses, but since 1995 she's been working on her own empire – now encompassing nine stores, including three in Belgium. Her well-priced creations feature mainly solid colours, floaty, layered separates and dresses in linen, cotton and wool. (625 12 84; www.corakemperman.nl; Leidsestraat 72; 1/2/5 Prinsengracht)

Filippa K
CLOTHING

45 Map p70, C2

Dutch film luminary Carice van Houten has been spotted shopping here, so why shouldn't you? A favourite of local designers, Filippa K is one of the top Scandinavian designers worldwide; wearing one of her glam-yet-functional dresses or ensembles guarantees compliments as well as comfort. (www.filippa-k.com; Leidsestraat 53; 1/2/5 Prinsengracht)

Tinkerbell
CHILDREN'S

46 Map p70, C3

The mechanical bear blowing bubbles outside this shop fascinates kids, as do the intriguing technical and scientific toys inside. You'll also find historical costumes, plush toys and an entire section for babies. (www.tinkerbelltoys.nl; Spiegelgracht 10; 7/10 Spiegelgracht)

Local Life
Utrechtsestraat

A stone's throw south from gaudy Rembrandtplein, **Utrechtsestraat** is a relaxed artery stocked with enticing shops, designer bars and cosy eateries – a prime place to wander (assuming the 2012 road construction gets completed) and discover a great local hang-out. The street's southern end used to terminate at the Utrechtse Poort, a gate to the nearby city of Utrecht, hence the name.

Explore

Vondelpark & Old South

Often called the Museum Quarter, the Old South holds the top-draw Van Gogh, Stedelijk and Rijksmuseum collections. It's one of Amsterdam's richest neighbourhoods, and impressive manors rise on the leafy streets. Vondelpark is the city's bucolic playground next door, where joggers, picnickers, dope smokers, accordion players and frolicking children all cheerfully coexist.

The Sights in a Day

☀ Take a spin around beloved **Vondelpark** (p92). Long and thin – about 1.5km long and 300m wide – it's easy to explore via a morning jaunt. **Café Vertigo** (p98), **'t Blauwe Theehuis** (p99) and other eateries in the park offer sustenance. You'll see a great slice of freewheeling Amsterdam lifehanging out here.

☼ Pay homage to the arts in the afternoon (when crowds are lighter). Fortify with a meaty lunch at **Loetje** (p96) in the Old South, then hit the trail around the Museumplein. You'll likely have the stamina for just the **Van Gogh Museum** (p86) and **Rijksmuseum** (p90), but kudos if you fit in the modern **Stedelijk Museum** (p95) as well. They're all lined up in a walkable row.

☾ The streets around Overtoom burst with stylish ethnic eateries. For dinner go Moroccan at **Paloma Blanca** (p96), Ethiopian at **Lalibela** (p96) or Indonesian at **Blue Pepper** (p96). Afterward get cultured under the stars at Vondelpark's free **Openluchttheater** (p100), or listen to classical music soar in the pristine acoustics of the **Concertgebouw** (p100).

◉ Top Sights

Van Gogh Museum (p86)

Rijksmuseum (p90)

Vondelpark (p92)

♥ Best of Amsterdam

Museums

Stedelijk Museum (p95)

Eating

La Falote (p96)

Blue Pepper (p96)

De Peper (p98)

Entertainment

Concertgebouw (p100)

OCCII (p101)

Drinking

't Blauwe Theehuis (p99)

Getting There

🚊 **Tram** Trams 2 and 5 run from the city centre and make stops at the front entrance of the Vondelpark and at the museums around the Museumplein. Tram 1 is handy for attractions deeper within the Vondelpark and the bars and restaurants along Overtoom.

Top Sights
Van Gogh Museum

Housing the world's largest collection by artist Vincent van Gogh, the museum is as much a tour through the driven painter's troubled mind as it is a tour through his body of work. More than 200 canvases are arranged chronologically, starting with his early career in dreary Holland and ending less than a decade later in sunny France, where he produced his best-known work with his characteristic giddy colour. The museum opened in 1973 to house the collection of Vincent's younger brother Theo. Gerrit Rietveld, the seminal Dutch architect, designed the main building.

Map p94, D3

www.vangoghmuseum.nl

Paulus Potterstraat 7

adult/child €14/free, audio tour €5

10am-6pm Sat-Thu, to 10pm Fri

2/3/5/12 Van Baerlestraat

Van Gogh Museum, designed by Gerrit Rietveld

Don't Miss

Floor 1's Bounty

Let's cut to the quick: the museum's best stuff is on Floor 1 (not to be confused with Floor 0, aka the ground floor, which is where you enter). Floor 1 hangs Van Gogh's greatest hits, and it does so sequentially as you move clockwise from the main stairs. (Note if you're visiting prior to May 2013: the collection is on display at the Hermitage Amsterdam due to building renovation.)

Earliest Works (1883–85)

The room with Van Gogh's earliest works is filled with shadowy, sombre works from his time in the Dutch countryside and in Antwerp. He was particularly obsessed with peasants and 'painting dark that is nevertheless light'. *The Potato Eaters* (1885) is his most famous work from this period. *Still Life with Bible* (1885) shows his religious inclination. The burnt-out candle is said to represent the recent death of his father, who was a Protestant minister. *Skeleton with Burning Cigarette* (1886) was painted when Van Gogh was a student at Antwerp's art academy.

Paris Self-Portraits (1886–87)

In March 1886 Van Gogh moved to Paris, where his brother Theo was working as an art dealer. There his palette changed under the influence of the Impressionists. Dip into the Paris room and check out the many self-portraits. Van Gogh wanted to master the art of portraiture, but was too poor to pay for models.

Sunflowers in Arles (1888–89)

In 1888 Van Gogh left for Arles in Provence to delve into its colourful landscapes. The room devoted to this period hangs an awesome line-up of *Sunflowers* (1889) and other blossoms. Also here

JEAN-PIERRE LESCOURRET / GETTY IMAGES ©

☑ Top Tips

▸ Entrance queues can be long. Try waiting until after 3pm.

▸ Discount cards and prebooked tickets expedite the process. I Amsterdam Card holders have a separate 'fast' lane for entry. Advance ticket holders also get in more quickly.

▸ Advance tickets are available online or at tourist information offices, with no surcharge. They must be printed.

▸ Visit on Friday evenings, when the museum stays open late, serves drinks and hosts free cultural events.

✕ Take a Break

Hit the **Albert Heijn** (☎ 662 04 16; Van Baerlestraat 33a; ⏰8am-10pm; 🚊3/5/12/16/24 Museumplein) supermarket for picnic fixings to take out on the Museumplein. Or grab a table by the museum cafe's big windows, and snack on quiche and wine while overlooking the grassy square.

Understand
Rich Afterlife

While Van Gogh would come to be regarded as a giant among artists, he sold only one painting during his lifetime (*Red Vineyard at Arles*, in case you're wondering; it hangs at Moscow's Pushkin Museum). Fame didn't arrive until a few decades after his death, and Van Gogh has his sister-in-law Johanna (Theo's wife) to thank for it. Johanna came from a wealthy Amsterdam family and used her connections to promote Vincent's work. She did a heckuva job – his *Portrait of Dr Gachet* (US$82 million) and *Irises* (US$54 million) are among the most expensive paintings ever sold. It's a far cry from the 400 francs (US$1600) he earned on his lone paycheck for a canvas.

is *The Bedroom* (1888), which depicts Van Gogh's sleeping quarters at the house where he intended to start an artists colony with Paul Gauguin. 1888 is perhaps most notorious as the year Van Gogh sliced off part of his ear.

The Final Years (1889–90)
The last room on Floor 1 has paintings from Van Gogh's final years. He had himself committed to an asylum in St Remy in 1889. While there he painted several landscapes with cypress and olive trees, and he went wild with *Irises*. In 1890 he left the clinic and went north to Auvers-sur-Oise. One of his last paintings, *Wheatfield with Crows* (1890), is an ominous work finished shortly before his suicide.

Other Floors
The ground floor shows paintings mostly by Van Gogh's precursors, such as Millet and Courbet, though Vincent's work is sprinkled in. Floor 2 houses temporary educational exhibits and works on paper. Floor 3 hangs Van Gogh's contemporaries and those he influenced. This is another bountiful level, where you might spy landscapes by Monet and Gauguin, or a room full of French fauvists.

Exhibition Wing
Behind the main building, reaching onto the Museumplein, is a separate exhibition wing (opened in 1999) designed by Kisho Kurokawa and commonly referred to as 'the Mussel'. It typically hosts a blockbuster exhibition.

Man of Letters
Van Gogh also was a prolific letter writer. The museum has categorised all of his missives online at www.van goghletters.org. Bring your smartphone, and you can access them using the museum's free wi-fi.

Van Gogh Museum

Earliest Works/
Netherlands
& Antwerp
(1883–85)

The Potato Eaters

Still Life with Bible

Skeleton with
Burning Cigarette

Wheatfield
with Crows

Final Years/St Remy &
Auvers (1889–90)

Sunflowers,
The Bedroom

Paris Self-Portraits
(1886–87)

Irises

Sunflowers
in Arles
(1888–89)

Self-Portraits

Floor 1

Café

Van Gogh's
Precursors

Paulus Potterstraat

Main
Entrance

To Exhibition
Wing

Shop

Floor 0

Top Sights
Rijksmuseum

The Rijksmuseum is the Netherlands' premier art trove. After a 10-year renovation, it reopens in its entirety in spring 2013, splashing Rembrandts, Vermeers and 7500 other masterpieces over 1.5km of galleries. Feast your eyes on meaty still lifes, gentlemen in ruffed collars and vintage landscapes bathed in pale yellow light. Those visiting before the reopening can see the 'best of' collection exhibited in the Philips Wing.

National Museum

 Map p94, E2

www.rijksmuseum.nl

Stadhouderskade 42

adult/child €15/free 🚹

🕙9am-5pm

🚊2/5 Hobbemastraat

Rijksmuseum

Don't Miss

Rembrandt & Night Watch

Rembrandt is the Golden Age's most inexhaustible brush-man. His gigantic *Night Watch* (1642) shows the militia led by Frans Banning Cocq. The work is actually titled *Archers Under the Command of Captain Frans Banning Cocq*. The *Night Watch* name was bestowed years later, thanks to a layer of grime that gave the impression it was evening. It's restored to its original colours now.

Vermeer & Hals

Among Jan Vermeer's paintings, check out the dreamy *Kitchen Maid* (1658) for his famed attention to detail. See the holes in the wall? The nail with shadow? Frans Hals is another Golden Age great. He painted with broad brushstrokes and a unique fluidity. *The Merry Drinker* (1628–30) shows his style in action.

Delftware & Dollhouses

Delftware was the Dutch attempt to reproduce Chinese porcelain in the late 1600s. The museum displays scads of the delicate blue-and-white pottery, often painted with images of royalty. And while it may sound odd, seek out the dollhouses. Merchant's wife Petronella Oortman employed carpenters, glassblowers and silversmiths to make the 700 items inside, using the same materials as they would for full-scale versions.

Facade & Gardens

Pierre Cuypers designed the Rijksmuseum, which was completed in 1885. He planned Centraal Station four years later. Both buildings mix neo-Gothic and Dutch Renaissance styles. Don't forget to stroll the free gardens around the exterior, where sculptures and architectural fragments pop up amid the hedges.

☑ **Top Tips**

▶ Entrance queues can be long. Try waiting until after 3pm.

▶ Prebook tickets online or at any tourist information office, and you'll get fast-track entry. At press time there was no surcharge for advance tickets, though this might change.

▶ The museum has a free mini-outpost at Schiphol Airport. It's located after passport control between E and F Piers, and is open from 7am to 8pm.

✗ **Take a Break**

The arty **Cobra Café** (☎470 01 11; www.cobra cafe.nl; Hobbemastraat 18; mains €7-13; ⏱lunch & dinner; 🚊2/5 Hobbemastraat) on the Museumplein is touristy, but the 'Karel Appel Taart' sure hits the spot. Snack vendors line the sidewalk between the Rijks and Van Gogh museums, serving sandwiches, pancakes, ice cream and drinks you can take to their outdoor tables.

Top Sights
Vondelpark

New York has Central Park. London has Hyde Park. And Amsterdam has the lush urban idyll of the Vondelpark, where tourists, lovers, cyclists, backpackers, cartwheeling children and champagne-swilling revellers all come out to play. On warm weekends, an open-air party atmosphere ensues: some kick back by reading a book, others hook up with friends to share a spliff or cradle a beer at one of the cafes, while others trade songs on beat-up guitars. In short, it's pure magic.

Map p94, E2

www.vondelpark.nl

Stadhouderskade

⏱ 24 hr

🚊 2/5 Hobbemastraat

Cycling through Vondelpark

Don't Miss

Early History

The park is named after the Shakespeare of the Netherlands, poet and playwright Joost van den Vondel (1587–1679). The English-style grounds were laid out on marshland – a typically Dutch feat of drainage and landscaping – in the 1860s and '70s. If it feels like a picture-perfect playground for the bourgeoisie, that's because city planners designed it as such. They hoped it would soften the loss of the Plantage, the east-side park that became residential around this time.

Hippie History

During the late 1960s and early 1970s, Dutch authorities turned the park into a temporary open-air dormitory for the droves of hippies who descended on Amsterdam. The sleeping bags are long gone, but remnants of the era live on in the squats that fringe the park, such as OT301 and OCCII, now both legalised into underground cultural centres.

The Grounds

The park's 120 acres roll out ponds, lawns, gardens and winding paths that encourage visitors to get out and explore. While more than 10 million people per year converge on the green space, it never feels too crowded to enjoy.

Highlights

Follow the signs to the pretty rose garden in the middle of the park. Pablo Picasso's sculpture *The Fish* dots the landscape nearby. Neon-green parrots flit through the trees; once pets, they were released into the wild decades ago. And don't forget the cafes, teahouse and outdoor theater in the park.

☑ Top Tips

▶ The main entrance is at the top (northeast) of the park on Stadhouderskade. As you walk southwest, the path splits off to the left or right and makes a complete circle in either direction.

▶ Telltale iron gates mark several other entrances around the perimeter.

▶ The park's flat, winding paths are prime for pedalling. The closest bicycle rental shop is **MacBike** (www.macbike.nl; Weteringschans 2; 🚊1/2/5/7/10 Leidseplein) across the Singel from the main entrance.

▶ Check the schedule at the Openluchttheater (p100), an outdoor stage with free concerts.

✕ Take a Break

The terrace at Café Vertigo (p98) has prime seats for watching the Vondelpark scene. For something more architecturally kooky, 't Blauwe Theehuis (p99) sets up some 700 seats outdoors around its flying-sauceresque building.

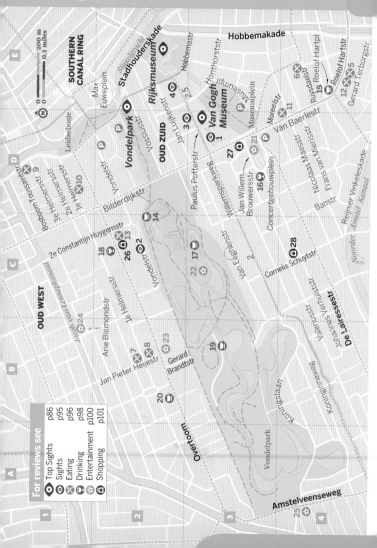

SOUTHERN CANAL RING

Hobbemakade

200 m
0.1 miles

Rijksmuseum

Stadhouderskade

Singelgracht

Max Euweplein

Leidsebosje

Vondelpark

Vossiusstr

OUD ZUID

Van Gogh Museum

Museumplein

Honthorststr

Idunastr

Roelof Hartpl

Gerard Terborgstr

Roelof Hartstr

Ruysdaelstr

Van Baerlestr

Moreelsestr

Paulus Potterstr

Jan Luijkenstr

Willemsparkweg

Concertgebouwplein

Jan Willem Brouwersstr

Nicolaas Maesstr

Frans van Mierisstr

Banstr

Reijnier Vinkeleskade

Cornelis Schuytstr

Noorder Amstel Kanaal

Bilderdijkstr

Vondelstr

2e Constantijn Huygensstr

3e Helmersstr

2e Helmersstr

1e Helmersstr

Boschoom Toussaintstr

OUD WEST

Jacob van Lennepkanaal

Arie Biemondstr

1e Helmersstr

Jan Pieter Heijestr

Gerard Brandtstr

Van Eeghenstr

De Lairessestr

Johannes Verhulststr

Vaertusstr

Nicolaas Verhulststr

Koningslaan

Overtoom

Vondelpark

Amstelveenseweg

Amsterdam

Sights

Stedelijk Museum
MUSEUM

1 ⊙ Map p94, D3

The Stedelijk is Amsterdam's weighty modern-art museum. Works by Monet, Picasso, Matisse and all the other 19th- and 20th-century stars hang here. Dutch homeboys Piet Mondrian, Willem de Kooning and Karel Appel also take pride of place. After a nine-year renovation, the museum reopened in late 2012 with a huge new wing (dubbed 'the Bathtub'). Ask at the front desk about free tours. (☑573 29 11; www.stedelijk.nl; Museumplein 10; adult/child €15/free; ◷11am-5pm Tue & Wed, 11am-10pm Thu, 10am-6pm Fri-Sun; 🚹; 🚋2/3/5/12 Van Baerlestraat)

House of Bols

Hollandsche Manege
RIDING SCHOOL

2 ⊙ Map p94, C2

Softly sunlit and smelling of hay and horses, the neoclassical Hollandsche Manege (1882) is an Amsterdam treasure. Buy treats in the shop to feed the creatures, or watch the instructors put them through their paces as you sip in the elegant cafe. To get there, enter through the long arcade on Vondelstraat, take a left turn and head up the stairs. (www.dehollandschemanege.nl; Vondelstraat 140; admission free; ◷10am-5pm; 🚋1 1e Constantijn Huygensstraat)

House of Bols
MUSEUM

3 ⊙ Map p94, D2

An hour's self-guided tour through this *jenever* (Dutch gin) museum includes a confusing sniff test, a distilled history of the Bols company and a cocktail made by one of its formidable bartenders, who train at the academy upstairs. It's kind of Tom Cruise *Cocktail* cheesy, but fun. Come Friday after 5pm, when admission is only €7.50. (www.houseofbols.com; Paulus Potterstraat 14; admission €12.50, 18yr & over only; ◷noon-5.30pm Sun-Thu, to 9pm Fri, to 7pm Sat; 🚋2/5 Hobbemastraat)

Diamond Museum

MUSEUM

4 Map p94, E2

Almost all of the exhibits at the small, low-tech Diamond Museum are clever re-creations, glinting in glass cases. Those who are economically minded might want to save money by just going next door to Coster Diamonds (the company owns the museum and is attached to it) and taking a free workshop tour, where you can see gem cutters and polishers doing their thing. (www.diamantmuseum.nl; Paulus Potterstraat 8; adult/child €7.50/5; ⏱9am-5pm; 🚊2/5 Hobbemastraat)

Eating

La Falote

TRADITIONAL DUTCH €€

5 🍴 Map p94, E4

Wee chequered-tableclothed La Falote is about Dutch home-style cooking, such as calf liver, meatballs with endives, and stewed fish with beets and mustard sauce. The prices are a bargain in an otherwise ritzy neighbourhood. And wait till the owner brings out the accordion. (🕿622 54 54; www.lafalote.nl; Roelof Hartstraat 26; mains €13-19; ⏱dinner Mon-Sat; 🚊3/5/12/24 Roelof Hartplein)

Loetje

TRADITIONAL DUTCH €€

6 🍴 Map p94, E4

This cafe's short menu may be written on the chalkboard, but everyone just orders thick steak, served medium-rare and swimming in delicious brown gravy. The staff are surprisingly good humoured, particularly considering the loud, meat-drunken mobs they typically serve. (www.loetje.com; Johannes Vermeerstraat 52; mains €15-25; ⏱lunch Mon-Fri, dinner Mon-Sat; 🚊16/24 Ruysdaelstraat)

Paloma Blanca

MOROCCAN €€

7 🍴 Map p94, B2

The name is Spanish, but the lanterns, dishware and mosaic-topped tables are straight out of a Marrakesh souk. Start with a gorgeous mezze platter before moving on to savoury mains of couscous and *tajine* (Moroccan stew) dishes featuring an array of meats, vegetables and fish. (🕿612 64 85; www.palomablanca.nl; Jan Pieter Heijestraat 145; mains €16-24; ⏱from 6pm Tue-Sun; 🚊1 Jan Pieter Heijestraat)

Lalibela

ETHIOPIAN €

8 🍴 Map p94, B2

Lalibela was the Netherlands' first Ethiopian restaurant and it's still a favourite. You can drink Ethiopian beer from a half-gourd, and sop up your stews, and egg and vegetable dishes using *injera* (a spongy pancake) instead of utensils. Trippy African music rounds out the experience. (www.lalibela.nl; 1e Helmersstraat 249; mains €8-12; ⏱dinner; 🚊1 Jan Pieter Heijestraat)

Blue Pepper

INDONESIAN €€€

9 🍴 Map p94, D1

Chef Sonja Pereira elevates Indonesian cuisine to art in her dramatic blue dining room. The exquisite *rijsttafel* (Indonesian banquet) includes an array of Pacific Rim–influenced dishes such as crackly crab, lamb saté, grilled scallops with tropical fruit, blue pears and coconut flan. Vegetarians options abound, too. (☎ 489 70 39; www.restaurantbluepepper .com; Nassaukade 366; set menus €53-70; ☻dinner; ⌖; ☒3/12 Overtoom)

Hap Hmm
TRADITIONAL DUTCH €

10 ☒ Map p94, D1

Elsewhere €8 might buy you a bowl of soup, but at this wood-panelled neighbourhood place, it might buy an entire dinner: simple Dutch cooking (soup, plus meat, veggies and potatoes), served on stainless-steel dishes. (www .hap-hmm.nl; 1e Helmersstraat 33; mains €8-11; ☻4.30-8pm Mon-Fri; ☒3/12 Overtoom)

Renzo's
ITALIAN €

11 ☒ Map p94, D4

Renzo's deli dishes out most of its pesto-y pastas, thickly cut sandwiches and omelettes for takeaway, though don't be shy about tucking in at the whitewood tables and benches on the miniterrace. (☎ 673 16 73; www.renzos .nl; Van Baerlestraat 67; items per 100g €1.50-3.25, ☻11am-9pm; ☒3/5/12/16/24 Museumplein)

Restaurant Elements
INTERNATIONAL €€

12 ☒ Map p94, E4

Students – the same ones who run the nearby College Hotel – prepare and serve contemporary international dishes at this mod restaurant. The result is white-glove service at an

---

Understand
The Golden Age

The Golden Age spans roughly the 17th century, when Holland was at the peak of its powers. It's the era when Rembrandt painted, when city planners built the canals and when Dutch ships conquered the seas.

It started when trading rival Antwerp was retaken by the Spaniards in the late 16th century, and merchants, skippers and artisans flocked to Amsterdam. A new moneyed society emerged. Persecuted Jews from Portugal and Spain also fled to Amsterdam. Not only did they introduce the diamond industry, they knew of trade routes to the West and East Indies.

Enter the Dutch East India Company, which wrested the Asian spice trade from the Portuguese. It soon grew into the world's richest corporation, with more than 50,000 employees and a private army. Its sister, the Dutch West India Company, traded with Africa and the Americas and was at the centre of the American slave trade. In 1672 Louis XIV of France invaded the Low Countries, and the brief era known as the Dutch Golden Age ended.

Local Life

Café Toussaint

On one of Amsterdam's prettiest streets, **Café Toussaint** (685 07 37; www.bosboom-toussaint.nl; Bosboom Toussaintstraat 26; sandwiches €5-7, mains €13-19; ⊙9am-10pm; 3/12 Overtoom) is a casual neighbourhood gem that feels like it's straight out of an Edith Piaf song. Come to sip cappuccino under the trees, or for creative twists on French classics in the candlelight evenings. It's carelessly sexy from noon to night.

excellent price. There are usually two seatings per night (5.30pm and 7pm). Reserve in advance. (579 17 17; www .heerlijkamsterdam.nl; Roelof Hartstraat 6-8; 4-course set menu €24.50; ⊙5.30-10pm Mon-Fri; 3/5/12/24 Roelof Hartplein)

De Peper   VEGAN €

This friendly restaurant at the OT301 arts complex (see 23 ✪ Map p94, B2) serves cheap, organic, vegan meals in a lovable dive-bar atmosphere. Sit at the communal table to connect with like-minded folk. Same-day reservations are required; call between 4pm and 6.30pm. (412 29 54; www.depeper .org; Overtoom 301; meals €7-10; ⊙7pm-8.30pm Tue, Thu, Fri & Sun; ; 1 Jan Pieter Heijestraat)

Overtoom Groente en Fruit   TURKISH €

13 🍴 Map p94, C2

Along with fruit and veggies, this Turkish grocery has a range of pre-made salads and snacks, including kebabs, and cheese-and-tomato-filled pitas – perfect for picnics in the park. It also sells chilled beer and sodas. (Overtoom 129; mains €3-5; ⊙from 8.30am Mon-Sat, from 10am Sun; 1 1e Constantijn Huygensstraat)

Drinking

Café Vertigo   CAFE

14 ☕ Map p94, C2

Of the Vondelpark's many cafes, Vertigo buzzes loudest. The terrace offers prime sunshiney seats to settle into, while swigging a brew and watching the action. It also prepares picnic baskets for takeaway. A cinema theme prevails inside (Vertigo is located in the old EYE Film Institute), with headshots of everyone from Ingrid Bergman to Dutch film star Carice van Houton on the wall. Service can be spotty. (www .vertigo.nl; Vondelpark 3; ⊙10am-1am; 🛜; 1 1e Constantijn Huygensstraat)

Wildschut   CAFE

15 ☕ Map p94, E4

This is a real gathering place for the Old South. When the weather's warm, pretty much everyone heads to the front terrace for a view of the surrounding Amsterdam School architecture. When skies are grey, soak up the atmosphere in the art deco interior. (Roelof Hartplein 1; ☉from 9am Mon-Fri, from 10am Sat & Sun; 🚊3/5/12/24 Roelof Hartplein)

Welling

BROWN CAFE

16 🚇 Map p94, D3

Tucked away behind the Concertge-bouw, this is a relaxed spot to unwind with a newspaper, sip a frothy, cold *biertje* (glass of beer) and mingle with intellectuals and artists. Don't be surprised if the cafe's friendly cat hops onto your lap. (www.cafewelling.nl; Jan Willem Brouwersstraat 32; ☉from 4pm Mon-Fri, from 3pm Sat & Sun; 🚊3/5/12/16/24 Museumplein)

't Blauwe Theehuis

CAFE

17 🚇 Map p94, C3

Did a flying saucer land in the park? That's what you might think as you approach this wacky structure, but it's simply a fabulous cafe surrounded by greenery. In summer the terrace is packed with seemingly everyone in town enjoying coffee and cake or cocktails and dinner. Ask for the pass-word to access the free wi-fi. (www .blauwetheehuis.nl; Vondelpark 5; ☉9am-10pm; 📶; 🚊1 1e Constantijn Huygensstraat)

Gollem's Proeflokaal

BEER CAFE

18 🚇 Map p94, C2

Take a day trip to Belgium without leaving Holland. Sip a cherry Kriek or a Trappist ale amid vintage beer signs

and paintings of tippling monks in Gollem's relaxed ambiance. Bartend-ers offer guidance to beer neophytes and fanatics alike. Dishes (€14 to €18), including Trappist cheese fondue, cro-quettes and Flemish stew, tempt drink-ers who work up an appetite. (www .cafegollem.nl; Overtoom 160-162; ☉from 4pm Mon-Thu, from noon Fri-Sun; 🚊1 1e Constantijn Huygensstraat)

Het Groot Melkhuis

CAFE

19 🚇 Map p94, B3

Like something out of a fairy tale, this huge thatched house at the forest's edge invites you in. The self-service cafe, with a vast drinking and dining forecourt, draws loads of families since it's next to a sandy playground where kids can go wild. (www.grootmelkhuis.nl; Vondelpark 2; ☉from 10am, closed Mon & Tue in winter; 👶; 🚊1 1e Constantijn Huygens-straat)

Parck

CAFE

20 🚇 Map p94, B2

Ah, the simple concepts in life: cold beer on tap and crave-worthy burgers (veggie ones, too) in a friendly corner pub stocked with oodles of magazines, a pool table, and plenty of outdoor tables and couch space for lounging. (www.cafeparck.nl; Overtoom 428; ☉from 3pm Mon-Fri, from noon Sat & Sun; 📶🍴; 🚊1 Jan Pieter Heijestraat)

Entertainment

Concertgebouw   CLASSICAL MUSIC

21 ⭐ Map p94, D3

Bernard Haitink, conductor of the venerable Royal Concertgebouw Orchestra, once remarked that the world-famous hall – built in 1888 with near-perfect acoustics – was the orchestra's best instrument. Free half-hour concerts take place every Wednesday at 12.30pm from mid-September until late June; arrive early. Those age 27 or younger can queue for €10 tickets 45 minutes before shows. Try the Last Minute Ticket Shop (www.lastminuteticketshop.nl) for half-price seats. (☎671 83 45; www.concertgebouw.nl; Concertgebouwplein 2-6; ⏲box office 1-7pm Mon-Fri, 10am-7pm Sat & Sun; 🚋3/5/12/16/24 Museumplein)

Openluchttheater   THEATRE

22 ⭐ Map p94, C3

Each summer the Vondelpark's intimate open-air theatre hosts free concerts and performances. It's a fantastic experience to share with others. Expect world music, dance, theatre and more. You can make a reservation (€2.50 per seat) on the website up to two hours in advance of showtime. (Open-Air Theatre; www.openluchttheater.nl; Vondelpark 5a; ⏲Jun-Aug; 🚻; 🚋1 1e Constantijn Huygensstraat)

OT301   ARTS CENTRE

23 ⭐ Map p94, B2

This graffiti-covered former squat in the old Netherlands Film Academy hosts an eclectic roster of bands and DJs, plus film screenings and theatre, with an emphasis on the strange and fringey. The centre offers yoga and dance classes, too. (www.ot301.nl; Overtoom 301; 🚋1 Jan Pieter Heijestraat)

SMART Project Space   CINEMA, ARTS CENTRE

24 ⭐ Map p94, B1

Once a pathology lab, this big brick complex is now a lab of a different sort, with experimental and art-house film in its two high-tech cinemas, plus avant-garde music in its auditorium. There's also a very good cafe, Lab111;

Stedelijk Museum (p95), designed by Benthem Crouwel Architects

periodically films are screened here too, and the menu reflects the movie. (☎427 59 51; www.smartprojectspace.net; Arie Biemondstraat 105-113; ☺from noon; 🚋1 1e Constantijn Huygenstraat)

OCCII

ARTS CENTRE

25 Map p94, A4

This former squat maintains a thriving alternative scene, and hosts underground bands, many from Amsterdam. There's also an anarchist library and a children's theatre. (☎671 77 78; www.occii .org; Amstelveenseweg 134; ☺closed mid-Jul–Aug; 👶; 🚋2 Amstelveenseweg)

Shopping

Pied à Terre

BOOKS

26 🔒 Map p94, C2

The galleried, sky-lit interior of this enormous yet elegant travel bookshop feels like a Renaissance centre of learning. If it's travel or outdoor-related, it's likely here: hiking and cycling tomes, gorgeous globes, travel guides and over 600,000 maps. Order a cappuccino and dream up your next trip at the cafe tables. (www.jvw. nl; Overtoom 135-137; ☺closed Sun; 🚋1 1e Constantijn Huygensstraat)

Broekmans & Van Poppel

MUSIC

27 🔒 Map p94, D3

Near the Concertgebouw (surprise!), this is the city's top choice for classical and popular sheet music, as well as music books. Head to the 1st floor for a comprehensive selection from the Middle Ages through to classical and contemporary. (www.broekmans.com; Van Baerlstraat 92-94; ☺Mon-Sat; 🚋2/3/5/12 Van Baerlstraat)

Van Avezaath Beune

FOOD & DRINK

28 🔒 Map p94, C4

Counter-staff in serious black aprons box up your chocolate-shaped *amsterdammertjes* (the bollards along city sidewalks) – a great (if phallic-looking) gift, assuming you can keep from eating them yourself. And if you do, well, there's plenty more chocolatey goodness beckoning from the glass cases. (www.vanavezaath-beune.nl; Johannes Verhulststraat 98; ☺closed Tue-Sat; 🚋2 Cornelis Schuytstraat)

Top Tip

Museum Shop at the Museumplein

The Van Gogh Museum and Rijksmuseum jointly operate the **Museum Shop at the Museumplein** (Hobbemastraat; 🚋2/5 Hobbemastraat), so you can pick up posters, notecards and other art souvenirs from both institutions in one fell swoop (and avoid the museums' entrance queues). While the selection is not as vast as the in-house stores, the shop has enough iconic wares to satisfy most needs.

Explore

De Pijp

With its narrow streets crowded by a lively mix of people – labourers, intellectuals, new immigrants, prostitutes, young urban professionals, gay and lesbian people, movie stars – De Pijp is often called the Latin Quarter of Amsterdam. Aside from the Heineken brewery tour, there aren't many sights. But free-spirited cafes and ethnic eats on every block? That's where De Pijp rocks it.

The Sights in a Day

☀ Check out the crazy-creative bicycles at **Fietsfabriek** (p112), then plot how you can get one shipped home while sucking down coffee at **Café de Groene Vlinder** (p110). It won't take long before the slew of multicultural street vendors along Albert Cuypstraat tempts. Note the shops behind the stalls as well – kitchen gadgets, bike locks, neat fabrics – anything goes.

☀ Have lunch at **Bazar Amsterdam** (p109). It offers a big, Turkish-tinged menu in a big, stained-glass ex-church. Then prepare for the **Heineken Experience** (p107), the multimedia brewery tour where you'll get shaken up, bottled and 'become' a beer. If you go in the late afternoon, the tasting at the end provides a built-in happy hour.

☽ You're absolutely spoiled for choice come dinnertime. There's **Mamouche** (p108) for sexy Moroccan, **De Waaghals** (p109) for funky vegetarian, **Balti House** (p110) for well-done Indian or **Firma Pekelhaaring** (p108) for unpretentious Italian. In the evening, catch a show at **CC Muziekcafé** (p112) or settle in for drinks at **Pilsvogel** (p111) or **Chocolate Bar** (p110).

For a local's day in De Pijp, see p104.

○ Local Life

Discovering Bohemian De Pijp (p104)

♥ Best of Amsterdam

Shopping
Albert Cuypmarkt (p104)

Eating
De Waaghals (p109)

Drinking
Kingfisher (p112)

Entertainment
Badcuyp (p105)

Parks & Gardens
Sarphatipark (p105)

For Kids
Taart van m'n Tante (p109)

Getting There

🚊 **Tram** Trams 16 and 24 roll down Ferdinand Bolstraat right by De Pijp's main sights, all the way from Centraal Station.

Local Life
Discovering Bohemian De Pijp

Artists and intellectuals have hung out in De Pijp since the 19th century, when the former slum's cheap housing drew them in. The district still wafts bohemian flair, from the spicy market at its epicentre to the cool-cat cafes and music clubs that jam its streets. A surprise red light area also makes an appearance.

① Albert Cuypmarkt

The half-mile-long **Albert Cuypmarkt** (www.albertcuypmarkt.nl; Albert Cuypstraat, btwn Ferdinand Bolstraat & Van Woustraat; ⏰10am-5pm Mon-Sat; 🚋16/24 Albert Cuypstraat) is Amsterdam's largest, busiest market. Here immigrants mix with locals, hawking rice cookers, spices and Dutch snacks like herring sandwiches and *stroopwafels* (two cookie-like waffles with caramel syrup filling). Graze as you gaze at the goods on offer.

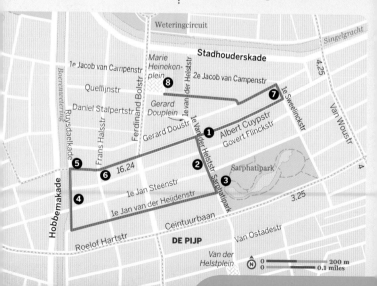

❷ Katsu

Flamboyant **Katsu** (www.katsu.nl; 1e Jan van der Helststraat 70; ⊘from 11am Mon-Sat, from noon Sun; 🚊16/24 Albert Cuypstraat), De Pijp's favourite coffeeshop, brims with colourful characters. The front table with newspapers lends a bookish vibe, although the smoke inside probably won't make you feel any smarter. Even if the coffeeshop ban for tourists is in effect, it's worth strolling by for a nostalgic sniff.

❸ Sarphatipark

While the Vondelpark is bigger and more famous, **Sarphatipark** (Centuurbaan; ⊘24hr; 🚊16/24 Albert Cuypstraat) delivers an equally potent shot of summertime relaxation, with far fewer crowds. In the centre you'll see a bombastic temple with a fountain, gargoyles and a bust of Samuel Sarphati, a resident who helped define the neighbourhood.

❹ Red Light Area

What the...? You're walking along Ruysdaelkade and suddenly there's a strip of **Red Light windows** between 1e Jan Steenstraat and Albert Cuypstraat. It's a good place to glimpse the world's oldest profession, minus the stag parties and drunken crowds that prowl the main Red Light District.

❺ Café Binnen Buiten

The minute there's a sliver of sunshine, **Café Binnen Buiten** (Ruysdaelkade 115; ⊘from 11am; 🚊16/24 Albert Cuypstraat) gets packed. Sure, the food looks good, and the bar is candlelit and cosy. But what really brings the crowds is the best canalside terrace in De Pijp, a terrific location for a lazy afternoon.

❻ Orontes

The chef at **Orontes** (📞679 62 25; www.orontes.nl; Albert Cuypstraat 40; mains €14-19; ⊘dinner Mon-Sat; 📞; 🚊16/24 Albert Cuypstraat) imports many of his ingredients from his Turkish homeland, and authentic flavours are the result. Charcoal-grilled meat, fish and eggplant dishes wow in their savoury simplicity. Check out nearby restaurants: Albert Cuypstraat is ground zero for exotic ethnic fare.

❼ Badcuyp

Combining a local vibe with top-notch international performers, **Badcuyp** (www.badcuyp.org; 1e Sweelinckstraat 10; tickets €4-8; ⊘Tue-Sun; 🚊4/25 Stadhouderskade) brings a shot of far-out energy to the neighbourhood. From free jazz sessions (2.30pm Sundays) to salsa nights, you can't walk out after an evening here and not feel the love.

❽ Barça

One of the hottest bars in De Pijp, **Barça** (www.bar-ca.nl; Marie Heinekenplein 30-31; 🚊16/24 Stadhouderskade) (themed like 'Barcelona in Amsterdam') is the heartbeat of Marie Heinekenplein. Hang in the posh plush-red and dark-wood interior, or spread out onto the terrace, glass of sparkling vino in hand.

Stadhouderskade

Sarphatikade

Singelgracht

Singelgracht

Mauritskade

Weesperzijde

Amstel

Amsteldijk

Oosteinde

Sarphatikade

Hemonystr

2e Jan Steenstr

2e Jan Steenstr

2e Jan van der Heijdenstr

Sint-Willibrordusstr

Van Woustr

Van Woustr

Frederiksplein

Tolstr

1e Sweelinckstr

Sarphatipark

Te Ilgenstr

Burgemeester

Pieter Lodewijk Takstr

DE PIJP

Lutmastr

Van Ostadestr

Rustenburgerstr

Kerkstr du Jardinstr

Weteringschans

Nicolaas Witsenstr

Den Texstr

2e Jacob van Campenstr

Gerard Doustr

Albert Cuypstr

Govert Flinckstr

1e Van der Helststr

Sarphatipark

Van der Helststr

Weteringcircuit

Nicolaas Witsenkade

Marie Heinekenplein

1e Van der Helststr

Gerard Douplein

Ceintuurbaan

1e Jan Steenstr

1e Jan van der Heijdenstr

Ferdinand Bolstr

Stadhouderskade

1e Jacob van Campenstr

Quellijnstr

Daniel Stalpertstr

Frans Halsstr

Roelof Hartstr

Cornelis Troostr

Boerenwetering

Ruysdaelkade

Hobbemakade

200 m
0.1 miles

Sights

Heineken Experience BREWERY

1 Map p106, B2

Heineken used to be brewed in this very building. Now it's a glitzy, self-guided multimedia tour, the high price slightly offset by the three beers along the way. A nice touch: you can visit the brewery's sturdy draught horses in their original stables. Allow 75 minutes for the tour, and expect crowds. Buying tickets online saves some money. (☏523 9435; www.heineken experience.com; Stadhouderskade 78; adult/child €17/13 (under 18 only with adult supervision); ⏰10.30am-7pm Jun-Aug, 11am-5.30pm Sep-May; ⛟16/24 Stadhouderskade)

De Dageraad ARCHITECTURE

2 Map p106, C4

One of the best Amsterdam School housing projects aside from Het Schip, 'The Dawn' is worth a visit if you're an architecture buff. It was developed between 1918 and 1923 for poorer families. The central structure, on PL Takstraat, is a dramatic curving staircase. Tours (€7.50 per person) are offered on the hour Friday through to Sunday between 11am and 5pm, departing from the office at Burgemeester Tellegenstraat 128 (at the corner of PL Takstraat). (Dawn Housing Project; Pieter Lodewijk Takstraat; ⛟12/25 Cornelis Troostplein)

KAREN FOLEY / DREAMSTIME.COM ©

Heineken Experience

Understand

Amsterdam School Architecture

When Amsterdam School architecture started around WWI, it was as much a political movement as an aesthetic one. Architects such as Pieter Kramer and Michel de Klerk were reacting to the decadent, elitist style of neo-Renaissance buildings like Centraal Station, but also to appalling housing conditions for the poor. Their fantastical public-funded housing projects resemble shells, waves and other organic forms; they were obsessive about details, designing everything down to the house numbers. Some details were a bit paternalistic and controlling – windows high in the wall were meant to deter leaning out and gossiping with neighbours – but in general the buildings were vast improvements. Stroll around De Dageraad, then visit the museum at Het Schip (see p65) near Westerpark.

Eating

Firma Pekelhaaring ITALIAN €€

3 Map p106, D3

Full of graphic-designer types having long lunches with wine, this joint offers an arty industrial vibe with loads of fun and little pretence. Social touches – like the communal table, strewn with magazines and board games to play over dessert – belie the focused attention on fresh Italian flavours. Kids will find a small stash of toys to play with. (www.pekelhaaring.nl; Van Woustraat 127-129; mains €5-10 lunch, €10-23 dinner; ☉10am-midnight; 🛜🚻; ☐4 Lutmastraat)

Mamouche MOROCCAN €€

4 Map p106, B2

Mamouche gets serious acclaim for its French-accented North African cuisine: think Morocco amid minimalism. The sleek design, with exposed flooring, mottled raw plaster walls and slat-beam ceilings, complements the changing selection of organic, seasonal *tajine* (Moroccan stew) and couscous dishes. It is one of De Pijp's most posh urban spots. (☏670 07 36; www.restaurantmamouche.nl; Quellijnstraat 104; mains €16-24; ☉dinner from 6pm; ☐16/24 Stadhouderskade)

Op de Tuin MEDITERRANEAN €€

5 Map p106, C4

This is the kind of breezy, informal neighbourhood restaurant where you can while away an evening snacking on an antipasti platter (let the chef decide on a mix of Mediterranean standards) or a beautifully prepared three-course meal, and fantasise that you live across the street. Many of the regulars do. (☏675 26 20; www.opdetuin .nl; Karel du Jardinstraat 47; 3-course menu €26-30; ☉from 4pm Tue-Sun; ☐3/25 2e Van der Helststraat)

De Waaghals
VEGETARIAN €€

6 🍴 Map p106, A2

The popular white-walled 'Daredevil' is stylish enough that even non-veggies may reexamine their dining priorities. The menu concentrates on one country each month – say, Thailand or Italy – plus a rotating array of inventive seasonal, organic dishes. Book ahead (it takes online reservations, too). (📱679 96 09; www.waaghals.nl; Frans Halsstraat 29; mains €13-19; ⏰5-9.30pm Tue-Sun; 🍴; 🚊16/24 Stadhouderskade)

Bazar Amsterdam
MIDDLE EASTERN €€

7 🍴 Map p106, C2

Beneath a golden angel in the middle of the Albert Cuypmarkt, this one-time Dutch Reformed church has fab-u-lous tile murals and 1001 Arabian lights to complement the cuisine: from Moroccan to Turkish, Lebanese and Iranian. Fish and chicken dishes please meat eaters; eggplant and portobello mushroom dishes gratify vegetarians. Come for the gigantic breakfast spread, or just for a beer and baklava. (www.bazaramsterdam.nl; Albert Cuypstraat 182; mains €8-15; ⏰11am-midnight Mon-Thu, 11am-1am Fri, 9am-1am Sat, 9am-midnight Sun; 🍴🚼; 🚊16/24 Albert Cuypstraat)

Burgermeester
BURGERS €

8 🍴 Map p106, A3

This sleek little bistro makes the finest burgers in town, bar none. It uses only organic beef (or lamb, felafel or fish), in huge portions that would pass as a main dish without a bun. Then come the toppings: feta, fresh mint, pesto, pancetta and more. You can also get a killer milkshake, but don't ask for chips or fries. (www.burgermeester.eu; Albert Cuypstraat 48; burgers €7-9; ⏰noon-11pm; 🚼; 🚊16/24 Albert Cuypstraat)

Café Volle Maan
CAFE €€

9 🍴 Map p106, B3

You can't go wrong for lunch or brunch at this airy, bilevel cafe right on Sarphatipark. Play a game of Scrabble near the sunny floor-to-ceiling windows while munching on cheese pancakes, good burgers or homemade soups like sweet potato and thyme. The apple tart rocks. (www.eetcafevollemaan.nl; Sarphatipark 4; mains €5-16; ⏰10am-1am Wed-Sat, 11am-1am Sun; 📶; 🚊16/24 Albert Cuypstraat)

Taart van m'n Tante
BAKERY & SWEETS €

10 🍴 Map p106, B2

One of Amsterdam's best-loved cake shops operates from this uber-kitsch parlour, turning out apple pies (Dutch, French or 'tipsy'), pecan pie, and wish-your-mother-baked-like-this cakes. Hot-pink walls accent cakes dressed like Barbie dolls – or are they Barbies dressed like cakes? (www.detaart.com; Ferdinand Bolstraat 10; items €4-7; ⏰10am-6pm; 🚼; 🚊16/24 Stadhouderskade)

Today's
ITALIAN €

11 🍴 Map p106, A2

This tiny deli-cafe functions as an impromptu Italian cultural centre, with snatches of Italian heard among the English, Japanese and Dutch being spoken by neighbourhood expats and longtime residents. They all know that chef Davide makes the most wicked focaccia and creative lasagnes (the pumpkin will knock your socks off) around. The house-made tiramisu is one of De Pijp's worthier sins. (www .facebook.com/todaysamsterdam; Saenredamstraat 26hs; items €4-8; ⏱1-8pm Tue-Sat; 🚊16/24 Stadhouderskade)

Balti House
INDIAN €€

12 🍴 Map p106, A3

One of the best-kept secrets in De Pijp is this friendly spot with its soothing interior. The classics – from a smooth butter chicken masala to fiery tandooris and biryanis – never disappoint, and the three kinds of Indian *rijsttafel* (banquet) present a worthy culinary adventure for the seriously hungry. (📞470 89 17; www.baltihouse.nl; Albert Cuypstraat 41; mains €13-21; ⏱dinner; 🍴; 🚊16/24 Albert Cuypstraat)

Drinking

Café Berkhout
BROWN CAFE

13 🍺 Map p106, B2

Once a derelict spot, this beautifully refurbished brown cafe – with its dark wood, mirrored and chandelier-rich splendour, and shabby elegance – is a natural post–Heineken Experience winddown spot. No matter how much beer you've swilled at the brewery, you can't miss Berkhout: it's right across the street. (www.cafeberkhout.nl; Stadhouderskade 77; ⏱from 11.30am; 🚊16/24 Stadhouderskade)

Café Sarphaat
BROWN CAFE

14 🍺 Map p106, C3

Grab an outdoor table along the Sarphatipark, tuck into a *croque monsieur* (grilled ham-and-cheese sandwich) and a frothy beer, and see if you don't feel like a local. This is one of the neighbourhood's most genial spots, with a lovely old bar that makes sipping a *jenever* (Dutch gin) in broad daylight seem like a good idea. (📞675 15 65; Ceintuurbaan 157; 🚊3/25 2e Van der Helststraat)

Café de Groene Vlinder
BROWN CAFE

Like Chocolate Bar down the block (see **15** 🍺 Map p106, B2), the 'Green Butterfly' strikes just the right balance between hip and *gezellig* (cosy). This makes it the perfect spot to go for a *koffie verkeerd* (coffee with lots of milk) in the warm wood interior before meeting up for a *biertje* (glass of beer) on the hopping patio. (www.cafedegroenevlinder.nl; Albert Cuypstraat 130; ⏱from 10am; 🚊16/24 Albert Cuypstraat)

Chocolate Bar
DESIGNER BAR

15 🍺 Map p106, B2

Chocolate isn't the draw here – it's the sleek vibe, buttery yellow walls and

Europop soundtrack. The candlelit bar makes this place feel like a night out even at noon: curl up with a cosy blanket on the patio on chilly days and pose with a fashion mag. At night, it's a scene. (www.chocolate-bar.nl; 1e Jan van der Helststraat 62a; ⊘ from 10am Mon-Sat, from 11am Sun; 🚊 16/24 Albert Cuypstraat)

Pilsvogel
BROWN CAFE

16 📍 Map p106, B2

The kitchen dispenses small plates (€3.50 to €5.50) to a crowd aged 20-something, but that's really secondary when you're sitting on De Pijp's most festive corner. A warm Mediterranean feel reigns at this casual tapas-bar–cum-pub with one of the neighbourhood's prime people-watching patios. (www.pilsvogel.nl; Gerard Douplein 14; 🚊 16/24 Albert Cuypstraat)

Het Paardje
BAR

17 📍 Map p106, B2

Single? Get on 'the horse'. On any given night the neighbourhood's hotties head here, whether fresh from a broken heart or from a football game. Equal-opportunity sexiness abounds. It's the see and be seen nexus of De Pijp's beautiful people. (✆ 664 35 39; www.facebook.com/hetpaardje; Gerard Douplein 1; 🚊 16/24 Albert Cuypstraat)

Café Krull
BROWN CAFE

18 📍 Map p106, B3

This sophisticated cafe always seems to be full of folks reading thick books and having intense conversations next

Café de Groene Vlinder

to the enormous windows. A communal table, 10 beers on tap and smiling bartenders spinning eclectic music make it ooze with effortless charm. (✆ 662 02 14; Sarphatipark 2; ⊘ from 3.30pm Mon-Thu, from 2pm Fri, from noon Sat & Sun; 🛜; 🚊 16/24 Albert Cuypstraat)

Gambrinus
BROWN CAFE

19 📍 Map p106, B4

Congenial bilevel Gambrinus, with its giant windows and sprawling terrace, boasts some of the best bar food in town, from lunchtime *broodjes* (sandwiches) to full-on dinner. With a clientele spanning from college-age to retirement-age, wisecracking bartenders and vintage fixtures, it's as cheerful as a candy store – which is exactly what it used to be in the old days. (www.gambrinus.nl; Ferdinand Bolstraat 180; 🚋 12/25 Cornelis Troostplein)

Entertainment

CC Muziekcafé

LIVE MUSIC

20 ⭐ Map p106, B4

De Pijp has long needed a place like this: a low-key yet buzzing little club that dishes up interesting live acts nightly – from reggae to soul to rock – along with zero attitude. Most shows are free, though a handful charge up to €5. (www.cccafe.nl; Rustenburgerstraat 384; 🛜; 🚋 12/25 Cornelis Troostplein)

Rialto Cinema

CINEMA

21 ⭐ Map p106, B3

This great, old cinema near Sarphatipark focuses on premieres, and shows

eclectic art-house fare from around the world. Note that foreign films feature Dutch – not English – subtitles. The bi-level, stylish cafe buzzes with pre- and post-cinema folks dissecting plot, theme and cinematography. (www.rialto film.nl; Ceintuurbaan 338; 🚋 3/25 2e Van der Helststraat)

Shopping

Fietsfabriek

BICYCLES

22 🔒 Map p106, A2

Wessel van den Bosch trained as an architect, and now he makes custom bicycles that are sold at this wild and crazy shop, one of several branches in Amsterdam. Come in and pick up a *bakfiets* (cargo bike), a *familiefiets* (bike with covered 'pram') or a stand-ard *omafiets* (one-gear city bike). Just browsing is a joy. (www.fietsfabriek.nl; 1e Jacob van Campenstraat 12; ⏰ 1-6pm Mon, 9am-6pm Tue-Fri, 10am-6pm Sat; 🚋 16/24 Stadhouderskade)

Tiller Galerie

ART

23 🔒 Map p106, A2

Intimate, friendly Tiller Galerie has works by George Heidweiller (check out the surreal Amsterdam skyscapes) and Peter Donkersloot (think fuzzy, magnificent portraits of animals and famous actors like Marlon Brando). Prints by the late Herman Brood round out the selection. (www.tiller galerie.com; 1e Jacob van Campenstraat 1; ⏰ Thu-Sun; 🚋 16/24 Stadhouderskade)

Local Life
Kingfisher

Kingfisher (www.kingfishercafe.nl; Ferdinand Bolstraat 24; ⏰ from 10am Mon-Sat, from noon Sun; 🚋 16/24 Stadhouderskade) is the hub of De Pijp's signature feel-good vibe. The communal table welcomes laptops, newspapers and lunching by day. By happy hour the place is kicking. It's a lot of locals' 'local', and as it's on one of De Pijp's main streets, it offers a great view of the neighbourhood's action (creative bicyclists are just the start).

Het is Liefde GIFTS

24 Map p106, B2

Come feel the love in this wedding shop, where all forms of romance and general festivity are celebrated. Browse oodles of wedding keepsakes and ephemera, including whimsical cake toppers in boy-girl, boy-boy and girl-girl couplings. Whether you're falling in love or recovering from heartbreak, Het is Liefde delights. (www.hetisliefde.nl; 1e Van der Helstraat 13-15; ⊙Tue-Sat; 🚊16/24 Albert Cuypstraat)

De Vredespijp HOMEWARES

25 Map p106, B2

Art-deco home-accessories and furniture shop meets tiny cafe with excellent home-baked goods. It's De Pijp's ideal rainy-day refuge. (www .vredespijp-artdeco.com; 1e Van der Helstraat 11a; ⊙closed Sun; 🛜; 🚊16/24 Albert Cuypstraat)

Stenelux GIFTS

26 Map p106, A2

Find a delightful collection of gems, minerals and stones in this longtime favourite shop, or buy a (surprisingly affordable) old fossil for that old fossil you left back home. Stenelux has a fascinating collection from this world and beyond (including meteorites). (✐662 14 90; 1e Jacob van Campenstraat 2; ⊙Thu-Sat; 🚊16/24 Stadhouderskade)

De Emaillekeizer HOMEWARES

27 Map p106, C2

Bright-hued De Emaillekeizer brims with appealing enamel treasures, including metal tableware decorated in pretty designs from China, Ghana and Poland. The Dutch signs, such as the unmistakeable 'coffeeshop' ones, make unique souvenirs. (✐664 18 47; www.emaillekeizer.nl; 1e Sweelinckstraat 15; ⊙closed Sun; 🚊4/25 Stadhouderskade)

Noor CLOTHING

28 Map p106, B2

There are so many women's clothing stores on the Albert Cuypmarkt, you could spend a week browsing the bargains. The affordable, modern fashion at Noor may make you want to skip the competition altogether. Don't miss the jam-packed sale rack. (✐670 29 16; Albert Cuypstraat 145; 🚊16/24 Albert Cuypstraat)

Raak CLOTHING

29 Map p106, B2

Near the Albert Cuypmarkt, you'll find unique, midpriced fashion and gifts by Dutch and Scandinavian designers. (www.raakamsterdam.nl; 1e Van der Helststraat 46; ⊙closed Sun; 🚊16/24 Albert Cuypstraat)

Explore

Oosterpark & Around

Oosterpark is one of Amsterdam's most culturally diverse neighbourhoods. Unlike De Pijp, it has seen only the tiniest bit of gentrification and it's not (yet) on any trend-watchers' radar – which is precisely what makes it interesting. The sights to see are off the everyday tourist path: the Tropenmuseum's global ephemera, a Moroccan and Turkish enclave, and some urban-cool bars.

M_AGULLO / DREAMSTIME.COM ©

The Sights in a Day

☀ Spend the morning yodelling, sitting in yurts and checking out Dutch colonial booty at the **Tropenmuseum** (p118). Strike out east from here down Eerste van Swindenstraat to find the **Dappermarkt** (p118). Reflecting the Oost's diverse immigrant population, it's a heart-warming mix of people, food and multipacks of socks.

☀ Continue east and the road eventually turns into Javastraat, where old Dutch fish shops and working-class bars sit adjacent to Moroccan and Turkish groceries. The exotic strip offers prime grazing; sweet tooths will appreciate the divine bakeries. Assuming you're still hungry, keep going and you'll run into Javaplein for lunch at rustic **Wilde Zwijne** (p118). Or chill out nearby at the cafe of **Studio K** (p121).

☾ Dinner in the greenhouse at **De Kas** (p118) is a one-of-a-kind meal: reserve ahead. Something mod will most likely be going on all night at either **Trouw** (p121) or **Canvas** (p120), two arty bar-club combos tucked in old warehouses. Then again, you could always fritter away the evening watching boats float on the Amstel at **De Ysbreeker** (p120).

💜 **Best of Amsterdam**

Eating
Wilde Zwijnen (p118)

De Kas (p118)

Drinking
De Ysbreeker (p120)

Museums & Galleries
Tropenmuseum (p118)

Parks & Gardens
Oosterpark (p120)

Getting There

🚊 **Tram** Tram 9 goes from the city centre to the Tropenmuseum. Trams 10 and 14 swing through on their east–west routes, as well.

Ⓜ **Metro** The Wibautstraat stop is a stone's throw from the mod bars at the Oost's southwest edge.

PLANTAGE

Nieuwe Keizersgracht

Plantage Middenlaan

Artis Royal Zoo

Nieuwe Kerkstr

Plantage Muidergracht

Westermanlaan

Roeterssstr

Nieuwe Prinsengr

Alexanderplein

Alexanderkade

Nieuwe Achtergr

Nieuwe Achtergr

Valckenierstr

Sarphatistr

Weesperstr

Nieuwe Achtergracht

Korte Amstelstr

Mauritskade

Valckenierstr

Spinozahof

Weteringschans

M Weesperplein

Muntendamstr

Sajetplein

M Zeldenruststr

Spreeksteen
Oratory Point

Rhijnspoorplein

Mauritskade

Oosterpark

De Schreeuw

Slavery
Memorial

3.7

Weesperzijde

7

Ruyschstr

Onze Lieve
Vrouwe Gasthuis

2e Oosterparkstr

Ruyschstraat

3e Oosterparkstr

1e Oosterparkstr

OOSTERPARKBUURT

Populierenweg

Wibautstr

Amstel

Amsteldijk

M Wibautstraat

9 10

Nobelweg

GV Aemstelstr

N 0   200 m
   0   0.1 miles

E

F

G

H

Mauritskade

Pieter Vlamingstr

Pontanusstr

Timorplein

⭐11

Borneostr

Von Zesenstr

Dapperstr

Bankastr

Commelinstr

Madurastr

Sumatrastr

1

DAPPERBUURT

Javastr

Wagenaarstr

1e Van Swindenstr

⊙2

Balistr

INDISCHE
BUURT

1e Atjehstr

❌3

Javaplein

⊗5

2e Van Swindenstr

Dapperplein

1e Atjehstr

🍴8

Pieter Nieuwlandstr

2e Atjehstr

Riaowstr

⊗6

Reinwardtstr

Insulindeweg

2

Molukkenstr

Wijttenbachstr

🚇 Muiderpoort

Linnaeusstr

Polderweg

3

22.65

4

Middenweg

15

Populierenweg

TRANSVAALBUURT

59

Kamerlingh Onneslaan

13
🛍

Park
Frankendael

⊗4

5

For reviews see	
⊙ Sights	p118
❌ Eating	p118
🍴 Drinking	p120
⭐ Entertainment	p121
🛍 Shopping	p121

Sights

Tropenmuseum
MUSEUM

1 ⊙ Map p116, D2

You could spend all day in this absorbing anthropology museum, watching Bollywood clips, peering into faux bazaar stalls and listening to hits on the Mexican jukebox. The museum began as a collection of colonial booty, so the areas covering former Dutch territory are particularly rich. (Tropics Museum; ☑568 82 15; www.tropenmuseum.nl; Linnaeusstraat 2; adult/child €10/6; ⊙10am-5pm Tue-Sun; ⍟; ☒9/10/14 Alexanderplein)

Dappermarkt
MARKET

2 ⊙ Map p116, E2

The larger Albert Cuypmarkt in De Pijp may be the king of street bazaars, but the Dappermarkt is a worthy prince. The Oost's cultural diversity shows in the whirl of people, foods and goods from sports socks to shimmering fabrics, all sold from stalls lining the street. (www.dappermarkt.nl; Dapperstraat, btwn Mauritskade & Wijttenbachstraat; ⊙10am-4.30pm Mon-Sat; ☒3/7 Dapperstraat)

Eating

Wilde Zwijnen
CONTEMPORARY DUTCH €€

3 ⊗ Map p116, H1

The name means 'wild boar' and if it's the right time of year, you may indeed find it on the menu. The rustic, wood-tabled restaurant serves locally sourced, seasonal fare with bold results. There's usually a vegetarian option, and chocolate ganache with juniper berries for dessert. Get here via Javastraat, which runs into Javaplein. Tram 14 stops right by it, too. (☑463 30 43; www.wildezwijnen.com; Javaplein 23; mains €18-21, 3/4 courses €29.50/35.50; ⊙lunch & dinner Tue-Sun; ⍟☑; ☒14 Javaplein)

De Kas
INTERNATIONAL €€€

4 ⊗ Map p116, F5

Admired by gourmets citywide, De Kas has an organic attitude to match its chic glass greenhouse setting – try to visit during a thunderstorm! It grows most of its own produce right here, and the result is incredibly pure flavours with innovative combinations. There's one set menu each day, based on whatever has been freshly harvested. Reserve in advance. (☑462 45 62; www.restaurantdekas.nl; Kamerlingh Onneslaan 3, Park Frankendael; lunch menu €37.50, dinner menu €49.50; ⊙lunch Mon-Fri, dinner Mon-Sat; ☑; ☒9 Hogeweg)

Roopram Roti
SURINAMESE €

5 ⊗ Map p116, E2

There's often a line to the door at this bare-bones Surinamese place, but don't worry – it moves fast. Place your order – lamb roti 'extra' (with egg) and a *barra* (lentil donut) at least – with the man at the bar, and don't forget the fiery hot sauce. It's some of the flakiest roti you'll find anywhere, super-delicious for takeaway or to eat at one of the half-dozen tables. (1e Van

Understand

Multiculturalism & Immigration Conflict

Scratch that vision of a metropolis of 6ft-tall blond people. With nearly half its population hailing from other countries, Amsterdam rivals much bigger cities for diversity. People from the Netherlands' former colonies, Indonesia and Suriname, form the largest minority groups. Other significant presences in the city are Turks and Moroccans, many second-generation. The first wave came over in the 1960s, when the government recruited migrant workers to bridge a labour gap. The remaining 170 or so nationalities recorded in Amsterdam's most recent census represent the rest of the globe.

Tensions

Since 2000, the Netherlands' historically tolerant policy toward migrants has been called into question. Pim Fortuyn, a right-wing politician, declared the country 'full' before being assassinated in 2002. Social tensions flared anew in 2004, when filmmaker Theo van Gogh – known for his anti-Muslim views – was shot and stabbed to death on a street by Oosterpark. In a city famous for its open-mindedness, what did it mean that a native Amsterdammer, albeit of foreign descent, was behind the crime? The national government responded in 2006 by passing a controversial immigration law requiring newcomers to be competent in Dutch language and culture before they could get a residency permit. Citizens from the EU, USA and Japan were exempt due to preexisting arrangements. This meant the policy mostly fell on immigrants from non-Western countries, including Morocco and Turkey.

Going Forward

While the national government has swung to the right and tried to curb immigration as part of its policies, Amsterdam still leans left. It is remarkably integrated compared with some other European capitals. Immigrants aren't relegated to suburbs; just walk around De Pijp and you'll hear five or 10 languages spoken. The city's multiracial character is a point of pride and, post-Theo, many Amsterdammers have scoffed at nationalist politicians such as MP Geert Wilders, the firebrand who likened the Quran to *Mein Kampf*. And Amsterdammers always seem ready to bond over commerce – the wildly diverse Albert Cuypmarkt in De Pijp and Dappermarkt in the Oost are two fantastic places to see this in action.

Swindenstraat 4; mains €4-10; ⏱2-9pm Tue-Sat, 3-9pm Sun; 🚊9 1e Van Swindenstraat)

Pata Negra

SPANISH €€

6 ✖ Map p116, E2

This colourful tapas joint dishes up delicious morsels, such as super-garlicky prawns, grilled sardines and other savoury treats. On Sundays it adds a big ol' potful of paella to the mix, which is a belly-filling bonus indeed. Another branch of the restaurant can be found on Utrechtsestraat in the Southern Canal Belt. (☎692 25 06; www.pata-negra.nl; Reinwardtstraat 1; tapas €6-12, mains €12-18; ⏱noon-11pm Sun-Thu, to 11.30pm Fri & Sat; 🚊3/7/9 Linnaeusstraat)

Local Life
Oosterpark

Oosterpark (s'-Gravesandestraat; ⏱dawn dusk) was laid out in 1891 to accommodate the diamond traders who found their fortunes in the South African mines, and it still has an elegant, rambling feel, complete with regal grey herons swooping around the ponds. On the south side, look for two monuments: one commemorates the **abolition of slavery** in the Netherlands in 1863; the other, **De Schreeuw** (The Scream), honours free speech and, more specifically, filmmaker Theo van Gogh, who was murdered here in 2004 (see p119).

Drinking

De Ysbreeker

BROWN CAFE

7 🍺 Map p116, A3

Pull up a chair on the terrace at this cafe on the Amstel and it's hard to decide whether to face the beautiful buildings or the gleaming river lined with houseboats. Inside stylish drinkers hoist beverages in the plush booths and along the marble bar. Lap up organic and local beers (such as de Prael) and bar snacks like lamb meatballs. (www.deysbreeker.nl; Weesperzijde 23; ⏱from 8am; 🛜♿; 🚊3 Wibautstraat)

Spargo

CAFE

8 🍺 Map p116, E2

So you've done Oosterpark – sought out all the monuments and found the wild parrots chattering in the trees – and now need a drink to replenish? Spargo's buzzy little terrace sends out its siren call from across the street. It pours several local Dutch brews, including Brouwerij 't IJ (the windmill brewery a short distance away). FYI, the cafe's sign looks like Spar90. (www.cafespargo.nl; Linnaeusstraat 37a; ⏱from 10am; 🚊3/7/9 Linnaeusstraat)

Canvas

BAR

9 🍺 Map p116, B5

Take the elevator to the 7th floor for this restaurant-bar-club. It's edgy and improvisational, and is the social centre for all the artists with studios in the building (the former Volkskrant newspaper office). The sweet views are heightened by the creative cocktails (say, a lemongrass martini or Japanese gin fizz). Music is varied, from vintage voodoo to hippie psychedelic, with jazz and funk, too. (www.canvasopde7e .nl; Wibautstraat 150; ⏰from 11am Mon-Fri, from noon Sat & Sun; Ⓜ Wibautstraat; 🚊3 Wibautstraat)

Trouw
BAR, CLUB

10 🍺 Map p116, B5

Trouw is housed in a former newspaper printing warehouse, where the printing press floor has been transformed into an industrial-chic restaurant serving snack-sized plates of organic, Mediterranean-tinged dishes. You can also have a drink on the sculpture-studded terrace. But Trouw is more known for its way-late club nights (with food served till 2am) and its salon series talks on culture, architecture and urban design. (📞463 77 88; www.trouwamsterdam.nl; Wibautstraat 127; ⏰dinner Tue-Sat, club Fri & Sat; Ⓜ Wibautstraat, 🚊3 Wibautstraat)

Entertainment

Studio K
ARTS CENTRE

11 ⭐ Map p116, G1

Sporting two cinemas, space for bands and theatre, an eclectic Greek-Spanish restaurant (open for lunch and dinner from Tuesday to Sunday) and a huge terrace, the Studio K is your one-stop shop for hip culture in the Oost. Drop in for a coffee, and you might wind up staying all night to dance… (📞692 04 22; www.studio-k.nu; Timorplein 62; 📶👤; 🚊14 Zeeburgerdijk)

Tropentheater
THEATRE

12 ⭐ Map p116, D2

Adjoining the Tropenmuseum, but with a separate entrance, this is like no place else in Amsterdam, with music, films and performances from South America, India, Turkey, Kurdistan and beyond. (📞568 85 00; www.tropentheater.nl; Linnaeusstraat 2, Tropenmuseum; ⏰closed Jul & Aug; 📶👤; 🚊9/10/14 Alexanderplein)

Shopping

De Pure Markt
MARKET

13 🔒 Map p116, F5

On the last Sunday of the month De Pure Markt sets up in Park Frankendael (near De Kas restaurant), with artisanal food and craft producers selling sausages, home-grown grapes and much more. Keep an eye out to the market's west for the community of garden plots with teeny houses on them. The owners sit out on sunny days with wine and picnic fixings. (www.puremarkt.nl; Park Frankendael; ⏰11am-6pm Sun Mar-Jun & Aug-Dec; 🚊9 Hogeweg)

Nieuwmarkt & Plantage

Nieuwmarkt is a district as historic as anything you'll find in Amsterdam. Rembrandt painted canalscapes here, and Jewish merchants generated a fair share of the city's wealth with diamonds and other ventures. Wealthy residents laid out the Plantage as a garden district next door. The green area now hosts a botanic garden, zoo, colourful tattoo museum and beer-making windmill.

The Sights in a Day

☀ Begin at **Museum het Rembrandthuis** (p124), the master's impressive home where he painted his finest works. Nearby **Gassan Diamonds** (p132) gives the bling lowdown via free factory tours. Those who prefer history to baubles can visit the **Joods Historisch Museum** (p131), which provides the backstory to the neighbourhood's role as the old Jewish quarter.

☀ Nosh on wood-oven-fired slices at **De Pizzabakkers** (p133), then spend the afternoon taking in the Plantage's many sights. Our pick goes to the eye-popping **Amsterdam Tattoo Museum** (p130), complete with jars of pickled, inked skin from 19th-century sailors. The **Hortus Botanicus'** (p130) time-hewn plants and the resistance exhibits of the **Verzetsmuseum** (p130) are also here. When happy hour rolls around, stroll over to organic beer-maker **Brouwerij 't IJ** (p134) and swill at the foot of an authentic windmill.

☾ Fork into contemporary Dutch cuisine at **Hemelse Modder** (p133) for dinner. Then take your pick of the cafes around Nieuwmarkt square or head down the road to **Café de Doelen** (p135) for a nightcap.

For a local's day in Nieuwmarkt & Plantage, see p126.

◉ Top Sights

Museum het Rembrandthuis (p124)

○ Local Life

Cafe-Hopping in Nieuwmarkt & Plantage (see p126)

♥ Best of Amsterdam

Museums & Galleries
Amsterdam Tattoo Museum (p130)

Verzetsmuseum (p130)

Eating
Latei (p133)

Hemelse Modder (p133)

Drinking
Brouwerij 't IJ (p134)

De Sluyswacht (p127)

Shopping
Waterlooplein Flea Market (p127)

Getting There

🚋 Tram Trams 9 and 14 go to Waterlooplein, the Jewish sights and onward to the Plantage. Trams do not go to Nieuwmarkt square, but it's a short walk from Waterlooplein.

Ⓜ Metro There's a stop at Nieuwmarkt, though it's easier to tram to Waterlooplein and walk to the square.

Top Sights
Museum het Rembrandthuis

You almost expect to find the master himself at Museum het Rembrandthuis, set in the three-storey canal house where Rembrandt van Rijn lived and ran the Netherlands' largest painting studio between 1639 and 1658. He bought the abode at the height of his career, when he was awarded the prestigious *Night Watch* commission. The atmospheric, tchotchke-packed interior gives a real-deal feel for how Rembrandt painted his days away.

Rembrandt House Museum

Map p128, B3

www.rembrandthuis.nl

Jodenbreestraat 4-6

adult/child €10/3

🕙10am-5pm

🚊9/14 Waterlooplein

Rembrandts on display, Museum het Rembrandthuis

Don't Miss

The House

The house dates from 1606. Rembrandt bought it for a fortune in 1639, made possible by his wealthy wife, Saskia van Uylenburgh. On the ground floor you'll see Rembrandt's living room/bedroom and the anteroom where he entertained clients.

Studio & Cabinet

Climb the narrow staircase and you'll come to Rembrandt's light-filled studio, laid out as though he's just nipped down to the kitchen for a bite to eat. Artists give demonstrations here on how Rembrandt sourced and mixed paints. Across the hall is Rembrandt's 'cabinet' – a mind-blowing room crammed with the curiosities he collected: seashells, glassware, Roman busts and stuffed alligators.

Etchings

The top floor is devoted to Rembrandt's famous etchings. The museum has a near-complete collection of them (about 250), although they're not all on display at once. Expect to see between 20 and 100 inky works at any one time, depending on the exhibition. Demonstrators crank up an oak press to show etching techniques several times daily.

Bankruptcy

The house ultimately caused Rembrandt's financial downfall. He was unable to pay off the mortgage, and in 1656 the household effects, artworks and curiosities were sold to compensate his creditors. It's thanks to the debt collector's itemised list that the museum has been able to reproduce the interior so authentically. Rembrandt lived the rest of his years in cheaper digs in the Jordaan.

☑ **Top Tips**

▶ Crowds are lightest right at opening time or after 3pm.

▶ You can buy advance tickets online, though it's not as vital here as at some of the other big museums.

▶ Pick up the free audio tour. It's available down the stairs past the entrance desk.

✕ **Take a Break**

Tables splash out of mosaic-trimmed **Tisfris** (www.tisfris.nl; St Antoniebreestraat 142; mains €4-9; ◷ 9am-7pm; 🚊 9/14 Waterlooplein) and over the canal, almost to Rembrandt's door. Pull up a chair and ask about the sandwich of the day.

Behind the museum, food vendors waft felafel sandwiches, *frites* and other quick bites around the periphery of Waterlooplein Flea Market (p127).

Local Life
Cafe-Hopping in Nieuwmarkt & Plantage

Thanks to Nieuwmarkt's action-packed plaza and the Plantage's garden district greenery, the area makes for lively and lovely strolling. Distinctive cafes are the bonus here: they pop up in rustic shipping warehouses, 17th-century lockkeeper's quarters, the turreted city gate, and just about everywhere in between. A flea market and funky arts centre add to the daily buzz.

❶ Fuel Up at Café Orloff

Join the ranks on the sprawling outdoor terrace at **Café Orloff** (www.orloff.nl; Kadijksplein 11; ⊙from 8am Mon-Fri, from 10am Sat, from 11am Sun; 🚌22/42/43 Kadijksplein), or head inside, where folks chat around the magazine-strewn communal table. The kitchen turns out light breakfasts and cornbread sandwiches during the day, and light dinners with plenty of French wine in the evening.

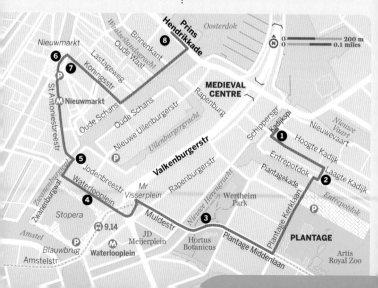

❷ Dockside Lounging at Entrepotdok

Entrepotdok (🚊9/14 Plantage Kerklaan) unfurls a 500m string of 19th-century shipping warehouses now packed with offices, apartments and dockside cafes perfect for lazing away a few hours by the water. Look closely across the water at the Artis Royal Zoo, and you might spot the oryx or zebras toward the east end.

❸ Wertheimpark's Memorial

Opposite the Hortus Botanicus, **Wertheimpark** (Plantage Parklaan; ⌚dawn-dusk; 🚊9/14 Mr Visserplein) is a willow-shaded spot brilliant for lazing by the Nieuwe Herengracht. On the park's northeast side locals often place flowers at the Auschwitz Memorial, a panel of broken mirrors installed in the ground that reflects the sky.

❹ Flea Market Finds

Covering the square once known as Vlooienburg (Flea Town), the **Waterlooplein Flea Market** (www.waterloopleinmarkt.nl; ⌚9am-5pm Mon-Sat; 🚊9/14 Waterlooplein) draws sharp-eyed customers seeking everything from antique knick-knacks to imitation Diesel jeans, pot lollipops and cheap bicycle locks. The street market started in 1880 when Jewish traders living in the neighbourhood started selling their wares here.

❺ Beer at De Sluyswacht

Built in 1695, **De Sluyswacht** (www.sluyswacht.nl; Jodenbreestraat 1; ⌚from 11:30am; 🚊9/14 Waterlooplein) lists like a ship in a high wind. The tiny black building was once a lockkeeper's house on the Oude Schans. Today the canalside terrace is one of the nicest spots in town to relax and down a Dutch beer (Dommelsch is the house speciality).

❻ The Multipurpose Waag

Dating from 1488, the ominous-looking **Waag** (www.indewaag.nl; Nieuwmarkt 4; ⌚10am-1am; Ⓜ Nieuwmarkt) was once a city gate, then a weigh house and now one of the many cafes that make surrounding Nieuwmarkt square a popular afternoon and evening hang-out. On Saturday a farmers market fills the plaza; on Sunday antiques take over the stalls.

❼ Fondue at Café Bern

Indulge in a dipping frenzy at delightfully well-worn **Café Bern** (📞622 00 34; Nieuwmarkt 9; mains €12-18; ⌚dinner; Ⓜ Nieuwmarkt). Locals have been flocking here for more than 40 years for the gruyère fondue and entrecôte. The cafe closes for part of the summer, when steamy weather lessens the hot-cheese demand. Reservations advised.

❽ Art at De Appel

See what's on at **De Appel** (📞625 56 51; www.deappel.nl; Prins Hendrikkade 142; adult/child €7/free; ⌚noon-8pm Tue-Sat, to 6pm Sun; 🚊4/9/16/24/25 Centraal Station), a swanky contemporary-arts centre that moved into the neighbourhood in 2012. The curators have a knack for tapping young international talent and supplementing exhibitions with lectures, film screenings and performances.

Damrak

Beurstr

Warmoesstr

Korte Niezel

Damrak

A

Zeedijk

Stormst

Gelderskade
Gelderseskade
Gelderseskade

Oude Waal

B

16

22

C

22,42,43

9

Prins Hendrikkade

Oosterdok

D

Onzudijs Voorburgwal

Onzudijs Achterburgwal

Bloedstr

18

Barndest

25

Koestr

23

Bethanienstr

Nieuwmarkt

11

15

NIEUWMARKT

Waalseilandsgracht

Binnenkant

Oude Waal

Lastageweg

Koningsstr

Peperstr

Rapenburg

12

MEDIEVAL CENTRE

Oude Hoogstr

Nieuwe Hoogstr

Nieuwmarkt

Keizersstr

Dijkstr

Oude schans

Oude Schans

Oude Schans

Nieuwe Uilenburgerstr

Uilenburgergracht

Nieuwe Uilenburgerstr

Zandstr

10

21

Raamgr

28

Museum het Rembrandthuis

Houtkopersburgwal

8

Valkenburgerstr

Anne Frankstr

Rapenburgerstr

Klovenierburgwal

Kloveniersburgwal

Kloveniersburgwal

20 26

Staalstr

29

Verversstr

Staalkade

Zwanenburgwal

Groenburgwal

Jodenbreestr

27

Waterlooplein

Mr Visserplein

Muldestr

Nieuwe Herengracht

Wertheim Park

Binnen Amstel

Amstel

Stopera

24

Blauwbrug

9,14

Nieuwe Amstelstr

5

Waterlooplein

6

JD Meijerplein

2

Hortus Botanicus

Amstelstr

Rembrandtplein

Amstel

Nieuwe Herengr

Nieuwe Herengracht

Hortusplantsoen

Weesperstr

Nieuwe Keizersgracht

0   200 m
0   0.1 miles

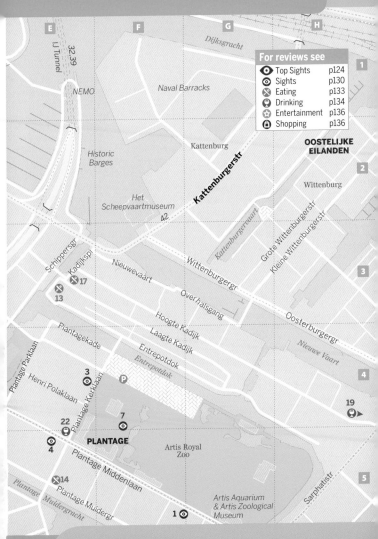

E F G H

IJ Tunnel
32.39

Dijksgracht

For reviews see
- ◉ Top Sights — p124
- ◉ Sights — p130
- ✖ Eating — p133
- 🍷 Drinking — p134
- ⭐ Entertainment — p136
- 🔒 Shopping — p136

NEMO

Naval Barracks

Historic Barges

Kattenburg

OOSTELIJKE EILANDEN

Het Scheepvaartmuseum
42

Kattenburgerstr

Wittenburg

Kattenburgervaart

Grote Wittenburgerstr
Kleine Wittenburgerstr

Schippersgr
Kadijkspl
✖17
✖13

Nieuwevaart

Wittenburgergr

Overhaalsgang

Oosterburgergr

Nieuwe Vaart

Piantagekade

Hoogte Kadijk

Laagte Kadijk

Entrepotdok
Entrepotdok

Plantage Parklaan
Henri Polaklaan

Plantage Kerklaan

◉3

P

19
🛒

22
🍷

7
◉

◉4

PLANTAGE

Plantage Middenlaan

Artis Royal Zoo

Sarphatistr

Plantage

✖14

Plantage Muidergr

Plantage Muiderlaan

1 ◉

Artis Aquarium & Artis Zoological Museum

Sights

Amsterdam Tattoo Museum

MUSEUM

1 ◉ Map p128, F5

This wild new museum has relics aplenty to back up its 'Tatican' nickname: the first electric tattoo machine, preserved pieces of tattooed flesh (check out the Boston whaler's skin from 1850) and painful-looking tribal implements from Borneo to Burma. Want a memento of your visit? Ascend to the 2nd floor, where resident tattoo artists apply the ultimate keepsake. (www.amsterdamtattoomuseum.com; Plantage Middenlaan 62; adult/child €10/5; ◷10am-7pm; 🚊9/14 Plantage Badlaan)

Hortus Botanicus

GARDEN

2 ◉ Map p128, D4

Established in 1638, the Hortus Botanicus was the repository for tropical seeds and plants Dutch ships brought back from exotic voyages. Groovy greenery includes the Palmhouse's 300-year-old cycad, one of the world's oldest potted plants; and a semicircular garden representing the entire plant kingdom. Guided tours (additional €1) of the compact grounds are held at 2pm on Sundays. (Botanical Garden; www.dehortus.nl; Plantage Middenlaan 2a; adult/child €7.50/3.50; ◷10am-5pm; 🚊9/14 Mr Visserplein)

Verzetsmuseum

MUSEUM

3 ◉ Map p128, E4

Intriguing exhibits detail how locals fought the German occupation during WWII. Learn how the illegal press operated and how thousands of people (like Anne Frank) were kept in hiding. It wasn't all noble: another chilling display articulates the reasons many citizens refused to shelter Jews. A smaller wing covers the Resistance in the Dutch East Indies. (Dutch Resistance Museum; ☎620 25 35; www.dutchresistance museum.org; Plantage Kerklaan 61; adult/child €8/4.50; ◷10am-5pm Tue-Fri, 11am-5pm Sat-Mon; 🚊9/14 Plantage Kerklaan)

Hollandsche Schouwburg

MEMORIAL

4 ◉ Map p128, E5

After 1942 this theatre became a detention centre for Jews awaiting deportation. Up to 80,000 people passed through on their way to the death camps. Glass panels show the names of the deported, and upstairs a modest exhibit hall displays photos and artefacts from the period; look for the heartbreaking tale of Bram and Eva Beem. (Holland Theatre; ☎626 99 45; www.hollandscheschouwburg.nl; Plantage Middenlaan 24; suggested donation €2.50; ◷11am-4pm; 🚊9/14 Plantage Kerklaan)

Amsterdam Tattoo Museum

Joods Historisch Museum

MUSEUM

5 ◎ Map p128, C4

A beautifully restored complex of four Ashkenazic synagogues from the 17th and 18th centuries reveals the history of Jews in the Netherlands. It vividly captures the vibrant Jewish community snuffed out by WWII. Pick up the free, English-language audio tour for extra insights. Admission tickets are in conjunction with the Portuguese-Israelite Synagogue. (Jewish Historical Museum; ☎626 99 45; www.jhm.nl; Nieuwe Amstelstraat 1; adult/child €12/3; ⊙11am-5pm; ⛵; ⌂9/14 Mr Visserplein)

Portuguese-Israelite Synagogue

RELIGIOUS

6 ◎ Map p128, C4

This was the largest synagogue in Europe when it was completed in 1675, and it's still in use today. The interior features massive pillars and some two dozen brass candelabra. Outside (near the entrance), take the stairs underground to the 'treasure chambres' to see 16th-century manuscripts and gold-threaded tapestries. Admission tickets also provide entry to the Joods Historisch Museum. (www.portugese synagoge.nl; Mr Visserplein 3; adult/child €12/3; ⊙10am-4pm, closed Sat; ⌂9/14 Mr Visserplein)

Zuiderkerk

Artis Royal Zoo
ZOO

7 ⊙ Map p128, F4

Artis has an alphabet soup of wild-life – alligators, birds, chimps and so on up to zebras – but the lush grounds are the true delight, full of ponds, statues and leafy pathways. Check out the aquarium's murky canal cross-section, featuring discarded bikes and creepy eels. If you prefer your nature stuffed, stop by the zoo's museum, a trove of taxidermy and other 19th-century relics. (📞523 34 00; www.artis.nl; Plantage Kerklaan 38-40; adult/child €19/15.50; ⏱9am-6pm Apr-Oct, to 5pm Nov-Mar; 👪; 🚊9/14 Plantage Kerklaan)

Gassan Diamonds
GUIDED TOUR

8 ⊙ Map p128, C3

This vast workshop demonstrates how an ungainly clump of rock is transformed into a girl's best friend. You'll get a quick primer in assessing the gems for quality, and see diamond cutters and polishers in action. The one-hour tour is the best of its kind in town, which is why so many tour buses stop here. Don't worry: the line moves quickly. (www.gassan.com; Nieuwe Uilenburgerstraat 173-175; admission free; ⏱9am-5pm; 🚊9/14 Waterlooplein)

Scheepvaarthuis
ARCHITECTURE

9 ⊙ Map p128, C1

The grand Scheepvaarthuis, built in 1916, was the first true example of Amsterdam School architecture. The exterior resembles a ship's bow and is encrusted with elaborate nautical detailing. Step inside (it's a luxury hotel now) to admire stained glass, gorgeous light fixtures and the art-deco-ish central stairwell. (Shipping House; Prins Hendrikkade 108; 🚊4/9/16/24/25 Centraal Station)

Zuiderkerk
CHURCH

10 ⊙ Map p128, B3

Famed Dutch Renaissance architect Hendrick de Keyser built the 'Southern Church' in 1611. The interior is now used for private events, but you can still tour the tower. Guides lead visitors up lots of stairs every 30 minutes, past the bells and to a swell lookout area for a sky-high city view. (www.zuiderkerkamsterdam.nl; Zuiderkerkhof 72; adult/child €7/3.50; ⏲1-5pm Mon-Sat Apr-Sep; **M**Nieuwmarkt)

Eating

Latei
CAFE €€

11   Map p128, B2

Young locals throng groovy Latei, where you can buy the lamps right off the wall (or the vintage chandeliers, or the tables, or any of the other mod decor – it's all for sale). The cafe goes ethnic (usually Ethiopian or Indian) for dinner Thursday through Saturday. Otherwise it serves sandwiches, apple pie and *koffie verkeerd* (milky coffee). (www.latei.net; Zeedijk 143; mains €6-16; ⏲8am-6pm Mon-Wed, to 10pm Thu & Fri, 9am-10pm Sat, 11am-6pm Sun; ✈; **M**Nieuwmarkt)

Greetje
CONTEMPORARY DUTCH €€

12   Map p128, D3

Elegant Greetje will make you re-consider Dutch cuisine. Never mind *stamppot* (mashed potatoes with veggies and bacon) – here you'll see dishes like leek soup, pickled mackerel and Dutch venison, all composed of market-fresh ingredients and beautifully presented. Sweet tooths can finish with the Grand Finale: a combo plate of six creamy, fruity, cakey desserts. (☎779 74 50; www.restaurantgreetje.nl; Peperstraat 23-25; mains €23-28; ⏲dinner; **M**Nieuwmarkt)

Koffiehuis van den Volksbond
INTERNATIONAL €€

13   Map p128, E3

What began life as a charitable coffeehouse for dockworkers was later revived by squatters. It still has a fashionably grungy vibe – wood floors, tarnished chandeliers and a giant red-rose mural. The ever-changing menu has huge plates of creative comfort food with dishes like red onion tart with blue cheese and lamb with artichoke puree. (www.koffiehuisvandenvolksbond.nl; Kadijksplein 4; mains €16-19; ⏲dinner; 🚋22/42/43 Kadijksplein)

De Pizzabakkers
ITALIAN €

14   Map p128, E5

'Pizza and prosecco' is the motto at this arty minichain, which means you sip the bubbly latter while waiting for the wood-oven-fired former. Generous toppings range from pancetta and mascarpone to ham and truffle sauce, though we're partial to the vegetarian with taleggio cheese, aubergine and zucchini. Be sure to take your ATM or credit card; the restaurant doesn't accept cash. (☎625 07 40; www.depizzabakkers.nl; Plantage Kerklaan 2; mains €7-13; ⏲lunch & dinner; 🚋9/14 Plantage Kerklaan)

Hemelse Modder
CONTEMPORARY DUTCH €€

15   Map p128, C2

Celery-green walls and blond-wood tables are the backdrop for light and unpretentious food, which emphasises

North Sea fish and farm-fresh produce. If there's no berry pudding for
dessert, the namesake *hemelse modder*
(heavenly mud) chocolate mousse is a
good fallback. The back terrace makes
for lovely al fresco dining. (📞 624 32 03;
www.hemelsemodder.nl; Oude Waal 11; mains
€23-27, 3-course menu €29.50; ⏰dinner;
Ⓜ Nieuwmarkt)

Lastage   FRENCH €€€

16 🍴   Map p128, B1

Small, cosy Lastage is another one
of those rose-among-thorns places.
The changing menu might start with,
say, stuffed guinea fowl atop red cab-
bage, followed by halibut with nutty
Camargue wild rice, beetroot puree
and saffron sauce. It's all beautifully
presented, and the elegant wine list
matches to a tee. (📞 737 08 11; www
.restaurantlastage.nl; Geldersekade 29;
set menus from €38; ⏰dinner Wed-Sun;
🚊4/9/16/24/25 Centraal Station)

🔍 Local Life
Tokoman

Queue with the folks getting their
Surinamese spice on at **Tokoman**
(Waterlooplein 327; sandwiches €3-4,
mains €7-9; ⏰11am-8pm Mon-Sat).
Chowhounds agree it makes the
best *broodje pom* (a sandwich filled
with a tasty mash of chicken and a
starchy tuber). You'll want the *zuur*
(pickled-cabbage relish) and *peper*
(chilli) on it, plus a cold can of coconut water to wash it down.

Café Kadijk   INDONESIAN €€

17 🍴   Map p128, E3

This sunny, split-level cafe looks like
it can serve no more than coffee from
its tiny kitchen, but in fact it does
quite good Indonesian food. Go for the
eitjes van tante bea (a spicy mix of egg,
shrimp and beans), as well as a mini
version of the normally gigantic *rijsttafel*
(Indonesian banquet). (www.cafekadijk.nl;
Kadijksplein 5; mains €12-18; ⏰4-10pm Mon,
noon-10pm Tue-Sun; 🚊22/42/43 Kadijksplein)

Toko Joyce   INDONESIAN €

18 🍴   Map p128, B2

Pick and mix a platter of Indonesian-
Surinamese food from the glass case.
The 'lunch box' (you choose noodles
or rice, plus two spicy, coconutty
toppings) is good value. To finish, get
a wedge of *spekkoek* (moist, layered
gingerbread). Take your meal upstairs
to the handful of tables, or outside,
where canalside benches beckon a few
steps from the door. (www.tokojoyce.nl;
Nieuwmarkt 38; mains €5-10; ⏰4-8pm Mon,
11am-8pm Tue-Sat, 1-8pm Sun; Ⓜ Nieuwmarkt)

Drinking

Brouwerij 't IJ   BEER CAFE

19 🍷   Map p128, H4

A de rigueur photo op, plus beer!
Amsterdam's leading microbrewery
happens to be tucked in the base of
De Gooyer Windmill, an 18th-century
grain mill and the last of five that

Waag (p127)

stood in this area. The organic house brews are excellent; try the *skeap-srond* (sheep's cheese) alongside. Tours (€4.50, including one beer) run Friday through Sunday at 3.30pm and 4pm. (www.brouwerijhetij.nl; Funenkade 7; ◷2-8pm; 🚊10 Hoogte Kadijk)

Café de Doelen   BROWN CAFE

20 Map p128, A4

Set on a busy canalside crossroads between the Amstel and the Red Light District, de Doelen dates back to 1895 and looks it: carved wooden goat's head, leaded stained-glass lamps and sand on the floor. But there's a fun, youthful atmosphere, and in fine weather the tables spill across the street for picture-perfect canal

views. (Kloveniersburgwal 125; ◷from 10am; 🚊4/9/14/16/24/25 Muntplein)

Café de Engelbewaarder   BROWN CAFE

21 Map p128, A3

Jazzheads will want to settle in at this little cafe on Sunday afternoon (from 4.30pm) for an open session that has earned quite a following. The rest of the week, it's a tranquil place to sip a beer by the sunny windows. (www.cafe-de-engelbewaarder.nl; Kloveniersburgwal 59; ◷from 11am; 🚊9/14 Waterlooplein)

Café Koosje   BROWN CAFE

22 Map p128, E5

If the three catchwords for real estate are location, location and location,

Tilted Architecture

No, you're not drunk... Amsterdam's buildings *are* leaning. Some – like De Sluyswacht (p127) – have shifted over the centuries, but many canal houses were deliberately constructed to tip forward. Interior staircases were narrow, so owners needed an easy way to move large goods and furniture to the upper floors. The solution: a hoist built into the gable, to lift objects up and in through the windows. The tilt allows loading without bumping into the house front.

then Koosje – located between the Artis Royal Zoo and the Hollandsche Schouwburg – has got a lock on the market. Perch yourself at the window or on the terrace to soak up the great corner vibe. (www.koosjeamsterdam.nl; Plantage Middenlaan 37; ⊙from 9am; 🚋9/14 Plantage Kerklaan)

De Bekeerde Suster   BEER CAFE

23 🍺 Map p128, B2

It has the brew tanks, it has the beautiful hardwood interior, it even has the history – a 16th-century brewery-cloister run by nuns. Stop in for a meal of pub grub to go with the house suds, or hoist a glass to start an evening on Nieuwmarkt. (www.de bekeerdesuster.nl; Kloveniersburgwal 6-8; ⊙from noon; Ⓜ Nieuwmarkt)

Entertainment

Muziektheater   CLASSICAL MUSIC

24 ⭐ Map p128, B4

Located in the odd, mod Stopera building (which is half *stadhuis*, or town hall, and half opera house), the Muziektheater is home to the Netherlands Opera and the National Ballet. Free classical concerts (12.30pm to 1pm) are held most Tuesdays from September to June in the Boekmanzaal. For a neat peek behind the scenes, take a building tour (€6) Saturdays at noon. (📞625 54 55; www .hetmuziektheater.nl; Waterlooplein 22; ⊙box office from noon, closed Aug; 🚋9/14 Waterlooplein)

Bethaniënklooster   CLASSICAL MUSIC

25 ⭐ Map p128, A2

This former monastery near Nieuwmarkt has a glorious ballroom, and is a great place to take in exceptional chamber music. Jazz fills the air on Tuesdays. (📞625 00 78; www.bethanien klooster.nl; Barndesteeg 6b; ⊙closed Aug; Ⓜ Nieuwmarkt)

Shopping

Droog   DESIGN, HOMEWARES

26 🛍 Map p128, A4

Droog means 'dry' in Dutch, and this design house's products are strong on dry wit. Check out inventions such as the 85-lamp chandelier, the cow chair,

and curtains with dress patterns.
Even small items, like superpowerful
suction hooks, are seriously smart.
(www.droog.nl; Staalstraat 7b; ☉Tue-Sun;
🚊4/9/14/16/24/25 Muntplein)

Het Fort van Sjakoo   BOOKS

27 🔒 Map p128, B4

Get the lowdown on the squat scene,
plus locally produced zines, anarchist
treatises and Trotsky translations, at
this lefty bookshop, which has been
in operation since 1977. Much of the
stock is available in English. (📞625
89 79; www.sjakoo.nl; Jodenbreestraat 24;
☉11am-6pm Mon-Fri, to 5pm Sat; 🚊9/14
Waterlooplein)

Henxs   CLOTHING

28 🔒 Map p128, B3

The two tiny floors of this indie
clothes store are crammed with fave
labels of skaters and graffiti artists,
such as Hardcore, Bombers Best,
Evisu and G-Star. Graffiti supplies
and edgy accessories are available in
Henxs' space next door. (www.henxs
.com; St Antoniesbreestraat 136; 🚊9/14
Waterlooplein)

Juggle   SPECIALTY SHOP

Just a short stroll down the block
from Café de Doelen (see 20 🚇 Map p128,
A4), wee Juggle puts more than mere
balls in the air: it also sells circus supplies, from unicycles to fire hoops to
magic tricks. (www.juggle-store.com;

Hortus Botanicus (p130)

Staalstraat 3; ☉Tue-Sat; 🚊4/9/14/16/24/25
Muntplein)

De Beestenwinkel   TOYS

29 🔒 Map p128, A4

From teeny-tiny teddy bears to pink
plastic pig snouts, this pleasantly
crowded shop sells *de best* (the best)
of *de beesten* (animals). Other bests:
plush toys from great toy makers,
lamps in animal shapes, and lots of
plastic reptiles. (www.beestenwinkel.nl;
Staalstraat 11; ☉10am-6pm Tue-Sat, noon-
6pm Sun & Mon; 🚊9/14 Waterlooplein)

Explore

Harbour & Eastern Docklands

In the past 15 years, the crumbling shipyard and warehouse district that used to be the city's fringe has morphed into a hub for cutting-edge Dutch architecture. The sparkling Muziekgebouw aan 't IJ and terrific maritime museum beguile, but mostly a visit here is about gawping at innovative structures. A scattering of bars and restaurants make the most of their dramatic waterfront locations.

JEAN-PIERRE LESCOURRET / GETTY IMAGES ©

The Sights in a Day

☀ Tick off the main sights in the morning. Take the escalators up to the top-floor cafe of the **Centrale Bibliotheek Amsterdam** (p143) for a great view of the cityscape (and optional breakfast). Walk over the bridge to wild-looking **NEMO** (p143), Amsterdam's kiddie-mobbed science center; another free vista unfurls from its terrace. Continue along the waterfront to **ARCAM** (p142) to stock up on architectural info. Then plunge into **Het Scheepvaartmuseum** (p142), the treasure-rich maritime museum.

☼ Spend the afternoon exploring the Eastern Docklands' odd, mod architecture. Pop into **Snel** (p145) for a sandwich to fortify. Then start wandering westward, past buildings like the huge angular silver one dubbed 'the Whale'. Cross the bridge to KNSM Eiland for drinks at **Kanis & Meiland** (p145) or **Kompaszaal** (p144), two cafes that are neighbourhood hang-outs. The latter sits in the former Dutch steamboat company arrivals hall.

☾ Reserve ahead for dinner at **Fifteen** (p143), celeb chef Jamie Oliver's do-good restaurant that trains underprivileged youth. Follow with an evening of music. The big-gun **Muziekgebouw aan 't IJ** (p146), jazzy **Bimhuis** (p146) and lower-priced **Conservatorium van Amsterdam** (p146) play notes nearby.

♥ Best of Amsterdam

Museums & Galleries
Het Scheepvaartmuseum (p142)

For Kids
NEMO (p143)

Centrale Bibliotheek Amsterdam (p143)

Entertainment
Muziekgebouw aan 't IJ (p146)

Bimhuis (p146)

Conservatorium van Amsterdam (p146)

Getting There

🚊 **Tram** Tram 10 has several stops in the docklands before ending its route on KNSM Eiland. Trams 25 and 26 go to the Muziekgebouw and the harbour's northeastern bits. It takes about 10 minutes to reach the neighbourhood from Centraal Station.

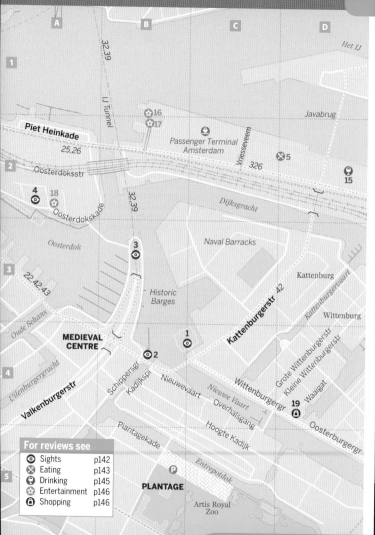

A

B

C

D

Het IJ

1

32.39

IJ Tunnel

☆16
☆17

Piet Heinkade

25,26

Passenger Terminal
Amsterdam

Javabrug

Vriesseveem

326

✖5

2

Oosterdoksstr

4 ⊙
18 ☆

Oosterdokskade

32.39

Dijksgracht

15 ♀

Oosterdok

3 ⊙

Naval Barracks

Kattenburg

3

22.42.43

Historic
Barges

Kattenburgerstr 42

Kattenburgervaart

Wittenburg

Oude Schans

**MEDIEVAL
CENTRE**

⊙2

1 ⊙

Wittenburgergr

Grote Wittenburgerstr

Kleine Wittenburgerstr

4

Uilenburgergracht

Schippersgr

Kadijkspl

Nieuwevaart

Nieuwe Vaart

Overhaisgang

Waaigat

19 🔒

Valkenburgerstr

Plantagekade

Hoogte Kadijk

Oosterburgergr

Entrepotdok

For reviews see	
⊙ Sights	p142
✖ Eating	p143
♀ Drinking	p145
☆ Entertainment	p146
🔒 Shopping	p146

P

PLANTAGE

Artis Royal
Zoo

5

E   F   G   H

N   0   500 m

0   0.25 miles

1

42

Java eiland

Sumatrakade

Javakade

KNSM-eiland

20   Surinamekade

21   7

9

IJ Haven

EASTERN DOCKLANDS

22

14   8

Levantkade

2

Veemkade

Oostelijke Handelskade

Lloydplein

10

11

12   13

Rietlandpark

23

3

CJk Van aalstrstr

65

Panamakade

26

26   Piet Hein Tunnel   26

43

OOSTELIJKE EILANDEN

Wittenburgervaart

Oostenburg

Borneolaan

4

Conradstr

Czaar Peterstr

Blankenstr

C van Eesterenlaan

Zeeburgerkade

6   Cruquiusweg

43,65

5

Zeeburgerpad

Singelgracht

Zeeburgerdijk   22

Sights

Het Scheepvaartmuseum
MUSEUM

1 ⊙ Map p140, C4

The Maritime Museum puts on a helluva display. In the Oost entrance you'll find nifty collections of globes from the 1600s, oodles of ship models, and silver and porcelain brought back from Dutch voyagers – all on the 1st floor. The 2nd floor has spooky ship figureheads and trippy timeworn navigation instruments. A full-scale replica of the Dutch East India Company's 700-tonne *Amsterdam* moors outside. (Maritime Museum; ☏ 523 22 22; www.scheepvaartmuseum.nl; Kattenburger-plein 1; adult/child €15/7.50; ⊙ 9am-5pm; 🚼; 🚌 22/43 Kattenburgerplein)

ARCAM
ARCHITECTURE

2 ⊙ Map p140, B4

This showpiece building of the Amsterdam Architecture Foundation should be the first point of call for architecture and urban design buffs. Exhibits vary, but you are sure to find books, guide maps and suggestions for tours on foot, by bike and by public transport. Check the website for digital resources and free apps about the city's buildings. (Stichting Architectuur Centrum Amsterdam; ☏ 620 48 78; www.arcam.nl; Prins Hendrikkade 600; admission free; ⊙ 1-5pm Tue-Sat; 🚌 32/33/34/35/359/361/363 IJ-Tunnel)

LONELY PLANET / GETTY IMAGES ©

NEMO

NEMO
MUSEUM

3 ⊙ Map p140, B3

Jutting into the harbour like a ship, Renzo Piano's stunning green-copper edifice is an excellent science and technology museum with hands-on laboratories. Kids will learn from exhibits like drawing with a laser, 'antigravity' trick mirrors and more. For adults, NEMO's stepped roof (admission free) is the city's largest summer terrace and worth a stair climb for the fantastic view. (☏531 32 33; www.e-nemo.nl; Oosterdok 2; admission €13.50; ⊙10am-5pm, closed Mon Sep-May; ; ☐32/33/34/35/359/361/363 IJ-Tunnel)

Centrale Bibliotheek Amsterdam
LIBRARY

4 ⊙ Map p140, A2

This nine-storey 'tower of knowledge' (its self-appointed nickname) is the country's largest library and has claimed a commanding spot in Amsterdam's increasingly modern landscape. Inviting chairs and couches are scattered around every floor, as are loads of internet terminals (per half-hour €1). The top-floor cafeteria provides terrific views over the city and water (you can go look without having to buy anything). (Amsterdam Central Library; ☏523 09 00; www.oba.nl; Oosterdokskade 143; admission free; ⊙10am-10pm; ☐25/26 Muziekgebouw)

Eastern Islands

The Eastern Islands – Kattenburg, Wittenburg and Oostenburg – comprise the area around Het Scheepvaartmuseum. They were constructed in the 1650s to handle Amsterdam's rapidly expanding seaborne trade. The Dutch East India Company set itself up on Oostenburg, where it established warehouses, rope yards, workshops and docks for the maintenance of its fleet. Private shipyards and dockworkers' homes dominated the central island of Wittenburg. Admiralty offices and buildings arose on the westernmost island of Kattenburg, and warships were fitted out in the adjoining naval dockyards that are still in use today.

Eating

Fifteen
INTERNATIONAL €€

5 ✕ Map p140, D2

'Naked chef' Jamie Oliver has brought to Amsterdam a concept he began in London: take 15 young people from underprivileged backgrounds and train them for a year in the restaurant biz. Results: noble intention, sometimes spotty execution. The setting, however, is beyond question: Fifteen faces the IJ, and the busy, open-kitchen space is city-cool, with graffitied walls and exposed wood beams. (☏509 50 15;

☑ Top Tip

Sightseeing from the Tram

For a bit of passive sightseeing, look no further than the tram: the lines rattle through great cross-sections of the city. One of the best routes is tram 10. It starts near Westerpark, swings around the perimeter of the canal loop and heads out to the Eastern Docklands, passing 19th-century housing blocks, the Rijksmuseum and Brouwerij 't IJ windmill along the way. Another good route is tram 5, starting at Centraal Station and cutting south through the centre of town.

www.fifteen.nl; Jollemanhof 9; mains €18-23; ⊙lunch Mon-Sat, dinner daily Sep–mid-Jul, dinner only Tue-Sat mid–Jul-Aug; 🚊25 PTA)

Gare de l'Est   INTERNATIONAL €€€

6 🍴 Map p140, G5

Gare de l'Est has both the smallest menu in Amsterdam and also the largest. It says that because four chefs (from culinary traditions spanning the globe) take turns nightly in the kitchen, what their course menus lack in length they make up for in variety. Portuguese tiles and glowing Middle Eastern lamps adorn the interior, and courtyard seating exudes good vibes. (📞463 06 20; www.garedelest.nl; Cruquiusweg 9; 4-course menu €32; ⊙dinner; 🚊43 Stadsdeel Zeeburg)

Kompaszaal   CAFE €€

7 🍴 Map p140, H2

Set in the century-old Royal Dutch Steamboat Company (KNSM in Dutch) arrivals hall, this airy cafe has a menu featuring Malaysian, Indian and Indonesian flavours. But the groovy green tiles and the water view from the balcony – a great spot for a beer – are even more captivating. On the ground floor, check out the scale models of the Eastern Docklands. (www.kompaszaal.nl; KNSM-laan 311; mains €15-20; ⊙11.30am-1am Wed-Sun; 🚊10 Azartplein)

De Wereldbol   INTERNATIONAL €€

8 🍴 Map p140, H2

A passionate and personable owner-chef, an ever-changing menu and a sweet view of bobbing boats on the water make this small, dark-wood restaurant a fine place to end a day of sightseeing in the area. Note the early closing time. (📞362 87 25; www.dewereldbol.nl; Piraeusplein 59; mains €17-21; ⊙5-9pm Tue-Sun; 🚊10 Azartplein)

Einde van de Wereld   VEGETARIAN €

9 🍴 Map p140, F2

At 'the end of the world', look for the big yellow-and-green boat *Quo Vadis*. The volunteer-run onboard restaurant is cheap and very cheerful. The set menu has one meat option and one vegetarian option. Show up early, because you can't reserve and when the food's gone, it's gone. Bands some-

times accompany the meal. (www
.eindevandewereld.nl; Javakade 61; meals €6-
9; ⏱from 6pm Wed & Fri; 🍴; 🚊10 Azartplein)

Odessa INTERNATIONAL €€€

10 🍴 Map p140, G3

A groovy boat that combines whimsy
and humour, with indoor and outdoor
eating decks and a 1970s-themed
'plush-porno' decor, Odessa is just
the sort of place where Hugh Hefner
would hold a debauched pyjama party.
As if to emphasise that fact, DJs take
over late at night. The menu changes
frequently, with an eye towards
simple steaks and fish. Book ahead on
weekends. (☎419 30 10; www.de-odessa.nl;
Veemkade 259; 3-course menu €34; ⏱dinner
Wed-Sat; 🚊10 C van Eesterenlaan)

Snel INTERNATIONAL €

11 🍴 Map p140, G3

We mention this restaurant not really
for a full meal, but as an excuse to
duck into the supremely cool Lloyd
Hotel, set in the shell of a 1920s brick
confection. The sunny restaurant
serves snacks all day, and has a great
back garden. (☎561 36 77; Oostelijke
Handelskade 34; snacks €4-7, mains €11-17;
⏱7am-1am; 🚊10 C van Eesterenlaan)

Café de Cantine CAFE €€

12 🍴 Map p140, G3

History buffs, come to feast on this
cosy cafe's bizarre past: in the 1920s it
was a quarantine house for emigrants
staying at the nearby Lloyd Hotel

who were shipping off to a new life in
the Americas. Luckily there's nothing
institutional about the eclectic food,
from savoury and sweet pancakes to
veggie tapas. (www.decantine.nl; Reitland-
park 373; mains €12-17; ⏱lunch & dinner; 🍴;
🚊10 C van Eesterenlaan)

Drinking

KHL CAFE

13 🚇 Map p140, G3

Proof of how far this district has
come, KHL is a one-time squatter cafe
gone legit. It's a historic brick building
with great tile work, and the garden
is worth a glass or two. There's live
music every Sunday evening – everything from Latin to pop to *klezmer*
(traditional Jewish music). (www.khl.nl;
Oostelijke Handelskade 44; ⏱Tue-Sun; 🚊10
C van Eesterenlaan)

Kanis & Meiland CAFE

14 🚇 Map p140, H2

A favourite among the 'islanders',
this cavernous spot has an inviting
wooden reading table, tall windows
facing the 'mainland' and a quiet terrace directly on the water. (www
.kanisenmeiland.nl; Levantkade 127; ⏱from
8.30am; 🚊10 Azartplein)

Café Pakhuis Wilhelmina CLUB

15 🚇 Map p140, D2

Well known for its hilariously fun
hard-rock karaoke as well as its

alternative dance nights, this is low-key clubbing (singing) at its best. (www.cafepakhuiswilhelmina.nl; Veemkade 576; ⚊25 PTA)

Entertainment

Muziekgebouw aan 't IJ

CONCERT VENUE

16 ⭐ Map p140, B1

This dazzling building plays host to everything from the Holland Symfonia (which typically accompanies the national ballet) to the prestigious Metropole Orkest, which does smart arrangements of jazz and pop. People under age 30 can get €10 tickets 30 minutes before showtime at the box office, or online via http://earlybirds.muziekgebouw.nl. Everyone else should try the Last Minute Ticket Shop (www.lastminuteticketshop.nl) for discounts. (📞788 20 00; www.muziekgebouw.nl, Piet Heinkade 1; tickets €26-37; ⏱box office noon-6pm Mon-Sat; ⚊25/26 Muziekgebouw)

✅ Top Tip

By Bike

Cycling is one of the best ways to explore the neighbourhood. MacBike's (www.macbike.nl) rental shop at Centraal Station is closest. From there it's a 10-minute pedal to the eastern districts.

Bimhuis

JAZZ

17 ⭐ Map p140, B2

The core of Amsterdam's influential jazz and improvisational music scene since 1973, the Bimhuis has kept its focus even after merging (architecturally) with the Muziekgebouw. Tuesdays at 10pm from September to June are an open jam session in the cafe – fun and free (as is the preceding music workshop at 8pm). (📞788 21 88; www.bimhuis.nl; Piet Heinkade 3; tickets €10-22; ⏱closed Aug; ⚊25/26 Muziekgebouw)

Conservatorium van Amsterdam

CLASSICAL MUSIC

18 ⭐ Map p140, A2

The city's prestigious music school, set in a dramatic building on the harbour, is a great place to see jazz, opera and classical performances, at very affordable prices. The snazzy venue has state-of-the-art acoustics, endless glass walls and light-flooded interiors. Check the program online or posted in the school's front window to see what appeals. (www.cva.ahk.nl; Oosterdokskade 151; ⚊25/26 Muziekgebouw)

Shopping

Frank's Smoke House FOOD & DRINK

19 🔒 Map p140, D4

Frank is a prime supplier to Amsterdam's restaurants. He learned how to smoke fish from the Swedes, and his excellent salmon, halibut, yellowfin tuna and eel can be vacuum-packed for easy passage through airport customs (which works, unlike with meat). You can also sit down at the single table and have an excellent mackerel sandwich or bowl of soup. (www.smokehouse.nl; Wittenburgergracht 303; ⏰9am-4pm Mon, to 6pm Tue-Fri, to 5pm Sat; 🚌22/43 Wittenburgergracht, 🚊10 1e Coehoornstraat)

Sissy-Boy
CLOTHING, HOUSEWARES

20 🔒 Map p140, H2

Never mind the name – Sissy-Boy is a Dutch chain that sells quirky print shirts and other items that tread the line between preppie and hip. This vast branch also stocks lots of home items and offers comfy chairs to sit in on the front porch. (☎419 15 59; www.sissy-boy.nl; KNSM-laan 19; ⏰9am-6pm Tue-Sat, 10am-6pm Sun & Mon; 🚊10 Azartplein)

Arrival/Departure
CLOTHING

21 🔒 Map p140, H2

This trendy shop, inspired by the world of skateboarding, offers an array of clothes, shoes, books, art and toys that bring out your inner rock-and-roll daredevil. Look for of-the-moment brands such as Ben Sherman, Stop Staring! and We are the Superlative Conspiracy. (www.arrivaldeparture.nl; KNSM-laan 301; 🚊10 Azartplein)

De Ode
SPECIALITY SHOP

22 🔒 Map p140, H2

Send your loved ones off in style, with a creative casket from this one-

Muziekgebouw aan 't IJ and the Bimhuis

of-a-kind shop. Open by appointment only, but a couple of interesting options are always on display in the window. (☎419 08 82; Levantkade 51; ⏰by appointment only; 🚊10 Azartplein)

JC Creations
CLOTHING

23 🔒 Map p140, H3

Take a deep breath when you enter this shop: classy corsets (for males and females) are the speciality. Plenty of ready-made options abound, but custom orders are welcome, too. (www.jc-creations.com; Baron GA Tindalstraat 150; ⏰Tue-Sat; 🚊10 C van Eesterenlaan)

The Best of
Amsterdam

Prinsengracht (p52)
SANDRA RACCANELLO/SIME/4CORNERS ©

Best Walks
Amsterdam's Splashiest Canals

🏃 The Walk

More canals flow in Amsterdam than in Venice. Get the camera ready, because this walk will go by some of the city's loveliest waterways. They're more than just a pretty picture, though. For more than four centuries the canals have kept Amsterdam above water, since they help drain the soggy landscape. Today 100km of channels do their duty. Romantic backdrops and groovy boating spots are a lucky bonus.

Start Corner of Staalstraat and Groenburgwal; tram 4/9/14/16/24/25 Muntplein

Finish De Ysbreeker; tram 3 Wibautstraat

Length 3km; two hours with dawdling

✖ Take a Break

Play the piano or board games amid the vintage-thrift decor at **Café Langereis** (see p78), a sweet spot at the foot of the Blauwbrug (Blue Bridge).

EYE35.PIX / ALAMY ©
Cruising the Keizersgracht

❶ Groenburgwal

Step out onto the white drawbridge that crosses the **Groenburgwal** and look north. Many Amsterdammers swear this is the loveliest canal view of all – a pick backed by Impressionist Claude Monet, who painted it in 1874 as *The Zuiderkerk (South Church) at Amsterdam: Looking up the Groenburgwal*.

❷ NAP Display

Head over to the Stopera building, Amsterdam's combination of city hall and **Muziektheater** (p136). Pop into the east entrance and check out the **Normaal Amsterdams Peil (NAP) display**. NAP is the Netherlands' sea level measurement, and the exhibit shows how much of Amsterdam falls below it.

❸ Blauwbrug

Cross the river via the 1884 **Blauwbrug** (Blue Bridge). Inspired by Paris' Alexander III bridge, it features tall, ornate street lamps topped by the imperial crown of Amsterdam, fish sculptures, and foundations shaped like the prow of a medieval ship.

❹ Reguliersgracht

Walk along the Herengracht to **Reguliersgracht** (p74), the 'seven bridges' canal. Stand with your back to the Thorbeckeplein and the Herengracht flowing directly in front of you. Lean over the bridge and sigh at the seven humpbacked arches leading down the canal straight ahead.

❺ Magere Brug

Walk along the Keizergracht and turn right toward the wedding-photo-favourite **Magere Brug** (Skinny Bridge). According to legend, two sisters built it. They lived on opposite sides of the river and wanted an easy way to visit each other. Alas, they only had enough money to construct a narrow bridge.

❻ Amstelsluizen

Continue south to the **Amstelsluizen**. These impressive locks, dating from 1674, allow the canals to be flushed with fresh water. The sluices on the city's west side are left open as the stagnant water is pumped out to sea.

❼ De Ysbreeker

Cross the river once more; take Prof Tulpplein past the InterContinental hotel to **De Ysbreeker** (p120). The building used to be an inn for the tough guys who broke ice on the Amstel so boats could pass. Take a seat on the enormous waterfront terrace to see what's gliding by these days.

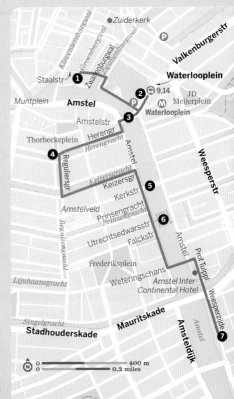

Best Walks
Cheese, Gin & Monuments

🏃 The Walk

This tour is a hit parade of Amsterdam's favourite foods and historic sights. Swoop through the Western Canals and City Centre, gobbling up traditional *kaas* (cheese), *haring* (herring) and *jenever* (gin) in between stops at the city's birthplace and its Royal Palace. It's a big bite of Amsterdam in under two hours. The best time to trek is early afternoon, when opening times for sights and bars coincide.

Start De Kaaskamer, tram 1/2/5 Spui

Finish Wynand Fockink, tram 4/9/16/24/25 Dam

Length 2km, 1½ to two hours with stops

✕ Take a Break

Inviting cafes and brainy bookstores ring the Spui (pronounced 'spow'; rhymes with 'now'), a broad square where academics and journalists hang out. **Hoppe** (see p34) has poured for the literati for over 300 years.

Dutch cheese

❶ De Kaaskamer

The Dutch eat more than 14kg of cheese per person annually and it appears much of that hunky goodness is sold right here in **De Kaaskamer** (p61). Wheels of Gouda, Edam and other locally made types stack up to the rafters. Get a wedge to go.

❷ Begijnhof

As you make your way through the Spui, keep an eye out just past the American Book Center for a humble wood door. Push it open and behold the hidden community known as the **Begijnhof** (p28) surrounding two historic churches and gardens. Cross the courtyard to the other entrance.

❸ Civic Guard Gallery

From the Begijnhof turn north and walk a short distance to the **Civic Guard Gallery** (p28). Paintings of stern folks in ruffled collars stare down from the walls. Cross the gallery and depart through the Amsterdam Museum's courtyard restaurant onto Kalverstraat.

❹ Royal Palace

Kalverstraat leads you to the **Royal Palace** (p24), Queen Beatrix's pad, though she's rarely here, preferring Den Haag for her digs. The sumptuous interior deserves a look.

❺ Nieuwe Kerk

The palace's neighbour is the **Nieuwe Kerk** (p29), the stage for Dutch coronations. After admiring its grandeur, get onto crowded Nieuwendijk and walk for a short while until you dive down Zoutsteeg.

❻ Rob Wigboldus Vishandel

C'mon, stop being shy about eating raw fish. Try the famed Dutch herring at **Rob Wigboldus Vishandel** (p32), a wee three-table shop. Once sated, depart Zoutsteeg onto Damrak.

❼ Dam

Cross Damrak so you're on the Nationaal Monument side of the **Dam** (p28) – Amsterdam's birthplace. Wade through the sea of bikes to see the urns behind the monument, which hold earth from East Indies war cemeteries. Now follow the street leading behind the NH Grand Hotel Krasnapolsky.

❽ Wynand Fockink

'Sshh, the *jenever* is resting', says the admonition over the door at **Wynand Fockink** (p34). The Dutch-gin maker's tasting room dates from 1679. The barkeep will pour your drink to the brim, so do like the locals to prevent spillage: lean over it and sip without lifting.

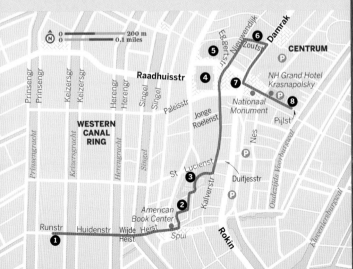

Best
Museums & Galleries

Amsterdam's world-class museums draw millions of visitors each year. The art collections take pride of place – you can't walk a kilometre without bumping into a masterpiece here. Canal-house museums are another local speciality. And, of course, the freewheeling city has a fine assortment of oddball museums dedicated to everything from tattoos to houseboats.

LONELY PLANET / GETTY IMAGES ©

All the Art

The Dutch Masters helped spawn the prolific art collections around town. You've probably heard of a few of these guys: Jan Vermeer, Frans Hals and Rembrandt van Rijn. They came along during the Golden Age when a new, bourgeois society of merchants and shopkeepers were spending money to brighten up their homes and workplaces. The masters were there to meet the need, and their output from the era now fills the city's top museums.

Other Treasures

The Netherlands' maritime prowess during the Golden Age also filled the coffers of local institutions. Silver, porcelain and colonial tchotchkes picked up on distant voyages form the basis of collections in the Rijksmuseum, Amsterdam Museum, Het Scheepvaartmuseum and Tropenmuseum.

Canal-House Museums

There are two kinds: the first preserves the house as a living space, with sumptuous interiors that show how the richest locals lived once upon a time, as at Museum van Loon. The other type uses the elegant structure as a backdrop for unique collections, such as the Kattenkabinet for cat art.

☑ Top Tips

▶ Take advantage of e-tickets. Most sights sell them and there's little to no surcharge. They typically allow you to enter via a separate, faster queue.

▶ Queues are shortest during late afternoon and evening.

▶ The I Amsterdam Card (per 24/48/72 hours €40/50/60) can save money; get it at tourist information offices.

Best Art Museums

Van Gogh Museum Hangs the world's largest collection of the tortured artist's vivid swirls. (p86)

Rijksmuseum The Netherlands' top treasure house bursts with Rembrandts, Vermeers, Delftware and more. (p90)

Museum het Rembrandthuis Immerse yourself in the old master's paint-spattered studio and handsome home. (p124)

Stedelijk Museum Renowned modern art from Picasso to Mondrian to Warhol stuffs the newly revamped building. (p95)

Hermitage Amsterdam The satellite of Russia's Hermitage Museum features one-off, blockbuster exhibits. (p72)

FOAM Hip photography museum with changing exhibits by world-renowned shutterbugs. (p72)

Best History Museums

Anne Frank Huis The Secret Annexe and Anne's claustrophobic bedroom serve as chilling reminders of WWII. (p44)

Amsterdam Museum Whiz-bang exhibits take you through the twists and turns of Amsterdam's convoluted history. (p28)

Verzetsmuseum Learn about WWII Dutch Resistance fighters during the German occupation. (p130)

Best Offbeat Museums

Amsterdam Tattoo Museum Eye-popping array of inky artefacts, including pickled skin from 19th-century sailors. (p130)

Kattenkabinet A creaky old canal house filled with kitty-cat art, including a Picasso. (p69)

Houseboat Museum Get a feel for the compact, watery lifestyle aboard a 23m-long sailing barge. (p51)

Tassenmuseum Hendrikje An entire museum devoted to handbags, from 16th-century goatskin pouches to Madonna's modern arm candy. (p73)

Electric Ladyland Prepare for a trippy time at the world's first museum of fluorescent art. (p51)

Best Canal-House Museums

Het Grachtenhuis Walks you through the history of the 400-year-old waterways. (p50)

Museum Van Loon Opulent old manor whispers family secrets in its shadowy rooms. (p72)

Museum Willet-Holthuysen Sumptuous paintings, china and a French-style garden with sundial. (p72)

Best Underappreciated Museums

Tropenmuseum A whopping collection of ritual masks, spiky spears and other colonial booty. (p118)

Het Scheepvaartmuseum The Maritime Museum features ancient globes, spooky ship figureheads and a replica schooner to climb. (p142)

Museum Ons' Lieve Heer op Solder Looks like an ordinary canal house, but hides a relic-rich 17th-century church inside. (p30)

Best
Parks & Gardens

Amsterdam has around 30 parks, so you're never far from a leafy refuge. City planners built in green spaces from the get-go to provide relief from the densely packed neighbourhoods. They did a heckuva job. Enter the gates of Vondelpark or any of the other meadow-fringed landscapes, and you're hit with a potent shot of pastoral relaxation.

INGOLF POMPE / GETTY IMAGES ©

Best for Strolling & Picnicking

Vondelpark Amsterdam's premier green scene is a mash-up of ponds, lawns, thickets and winding paths beloved by kissing couples, free-wheeling cyclists and duck-chasing children. (p92)

Westerpark Abutting a former gasworks building turned edgy cultural centre, the west side's rambling, reedy wilderness has become a hipster hang-out. (p65)

Oosterpark Political monuments and grey herons dot the sweeping expanse, built for nouveau riche diamond traders a century ago. (p120)

Sarphatipark De Pijp's lush oasis of rolling lawns, statues and fountains is similar to Vondelpark but without the crowds. (p105)

Wertheimpark Laze under the willows by the canal, but don't forget to view the mirrored Auschwitz Memorial. (p127)

Best Gardens

Hortus Botanicus When Dutch ships sailed afar in the 1600s, the tropical seeds they brought back were grown in this wonderful garden. (p130)

Begijnhof Push open the unassuming door and voila – a hidden courtyard of flowery gardens appears. (p28)

Rijksmuseum Sculptures and architectural fragments pop up amid rose bushes and hedges in the museum's oft-overlooked gardens. (p91)

☑ **Top Tip**

▶ To compose a hearty picnic for Vondelpark, stop by Overtoom Groente en Fruit (p98). For Westerpark, several delis line Haarlemmerdijk and Haarlemmerstraat outside the park.

Museum Willet-Holthuysen An intimate French-style garden with sundial rolls out behind the gorgeous canal house. (p72)

Bloemenmarkt It's not a garden per se, but the flower market does grow and show colourful blooms aplenty. (p68)

Best
Canals

Amsterdammers have always known their Canal Ring, built during the Golden Age, is extraordinary. Unesco made it official when it dubbed the waterways a World Heritage site. As of 2013, the Canal Ring has been doing its thing for 400 years.

RICHARD WAREHAM / GETTY IMAGES ©

Best Views

Golden Bend (Gouden Bocht; Herengracht, btwn Leidsestraat & Vijzelstraat) Where the Golden Age magnates built their mansions along the regal Herengracht.

Reguliersgracht The tour-boat favourite 'canal of seven bridges', one of Amsterdam's most photographed vistas. (p74)

Best Canal Cruises

Boom Chicago Boats (www.boomchicago.nl; Leidseplein 12; per person €15; ☉tours 2.45pm; 🚊1/2/5/7/10 Leidseplein) The comedy club's 75-minute tours cater to a younger crowd; it uses smaller open-air boats (that can be covered in bad weather).

St Nicolaas Boat Club (www.amsterdamboatclub. com; Leidseplein 12) Also affiliated with Boom Chicago. Excellent tour in an open-air, 10-seat vessel that can manoeuvre into the narrowest canals. There is no set fee, just a suggested €10 donation. Alas, the club was on hiatus due to licensing issues at press time. Check the website for updates.

Canal Bus (www.canal.nl; day pass adult/child €22/11) Offers a unique hop-on, hop-off service; has 17 docks around the city near the big museums.

Blue Boat Company (www.blueboat.nl; Stadhouderskade 30; ☉every 30min 10am-7pm; 🚊7/10 Spiegelgracht) The main tour

(adult/child €14/7.50) clocks in at 75 minutes. Blue Boat also offers evening cruises, kids' cruises and art cruises in conjunction with the Rijksmuseum.

Canal Bike (www.canal .nl; per hour per person €8; ☉10am-6pm Apr-Oct, to 10pm in summer) Pedal boats to splash around the canals in at your own pace. Landings are by the Rijksmuseum, Leidseplein, Anne Frank Huis and the corner of Keizersgracht and Leidsestraat. Requires €20 deposit.

Best
Eating

No one sighs over Dutch food the way they do over, say, French fare. So we'll just call Amsterdam's hot global eats, from Indonesian rice tables to mod Moroccan plates to Basque *pintxos*, our little secret. Whatever you choose, meals here are something to linger over as the candle burns low on the tabletop.

Dutch Specialities

Traditional Dutch cuisine revolves around meat, potatoes and vegetables. Typical dishes include *stamppot* (mashed pot) – potatoes mashed with veggies (usually kale or endive) and served with smoked sausage or strips of pork. *Erwtensoep* is a thick pea soup with smoked sausage and bacon. *Pannenkoeken* translates as 'pancakes', although North Americans will be in for a surprise – the Dutch variety is huge and a little stretchy, served one to a plate and topped with sweet or savoury ingredients.

Indonesian & Surinamese Fare

The Netherlands' former colonies spice up local fare. The most famous Indonesian dish is *rijsttafel* (rice table): a dozen or more tiny dishes such as braised beef, pork satay and ribs served with white rice. Surinamese food features curries prominently. Roti are burrito-like flatbread wraps stuffed with curried meat or veg; they're delicious, filling and cheap.

Snacks

Vlaamse frites are the iconic French fries smothered in mayonnaise or myriad other gooey sauces. *Kroketten* (croquettes) are dough balls, with various fillings, that are crumbed and deep-fried; the variety called *bitterballen* are a popular brown-cafe snack served with mustard.

LONELY PLANET / GETTY IMAGES ©

☑ Top Tips

▶ Many restaurants, even top-end places, do not accept credit cards. Or if they do, they levy a 5% surcharge. Always check first.

▶ Phone ahead and make a reservation for eateries in the middle and upper price brackets. Nearly everyone speaks English. Many places also let you book online.

Best Dutch

Hemelse Modder North Sea fish with heavenly mousse for dessert. (p133)

La Falote Stewed fish, meatballs with endives and other daily specials

Herring sandwich, served traditional-style with onion and gherkin

of home-style cooking. (p96)

Moeders Comfort foods like mum makes; the sampler plate lets you try several types. (p54)

Wilde Zwijnen The Oost's rustic gem reaps praise for bold, eclectic seasonal fare. (p118)

Best Indonesian

Blue Pepper Many rank the Pacific Rim–tinged *rijsttafel* as Amsterdam's best. (p96)

Tempo Doeloe High-class *rijsttafel* without pretense, and one that knows how to fire up the spice. (p75)

Best Budget

'Skek Students serve thick-cut sandwiches and

healthy main dishes for bargain prices. (p33)

Latei Cute-as-a-button cafe by day goes global Thursday through Saturday with Ethiopian or Indian fare. (p133)

Van Dobben Meaty goodness diner-style. (p74)

Best Bakeries

Lanskroon One word: *stroopwafel*. (p33)

Gebr Niemeijer Flaky croissants and walnut bread/lamb sausage sandwiches amid the centre's head shops. (p33)

Best for Foodies

De Kas Dine in the greenhouse that grew your meal's ingredients (p118)

Gartine Slow-food sandwiches, salads and a dazzling high tea. (p30)

Marius The chef whips up dishes from his daily market-finds. (p65)

Best Vegetarian

De Waaghals The menu emulates a different country each month, but it's always veggie. (p109)

De Peper The OT301 squat cooks vegan meals for the masses. (p98)

Best French

Café Toussaint Join the local crowd lingering over omelettes and lattes. (p98)

Lastage Carve into exquisitely sauced fowl and fish with wine to match in cosy environs. (p134)

Best
Drinking

Despite its wild party-animal reputation, Amsterdam remains a cafe society, where the pursuit of pleasure is more about cosiness and charm than hedonism. Coffee, beer and Dutch gin fill local cups, each a fine companion for whiling away the afternoon on a sunny canalside terrace.

MARTIN CHILD / GETTY IMAGES ©

Brown Cafes

Bruin cafés (brown cafes) are Amsterdam's crowning glory. The true specimen has been in business a while and gets its name from centuries' worth of smoke stains on the walls. Brown cafes have candle-topped tables, sandy wooden floors and sometimes a house cat that sidles up for a scratch. Most importantly, brown cafes induce a cosy vibe that prompts friends to linger and chat for hours over drinks – the same enchantment the cafes have cast for 300 years.

Other Places to Drink

Grand cafes are spacious, have comfortable furniture and are, well, just grand. Designer bars are trendy with cool interiors. *Proeflokalen* (tasting houses) were once attached to distilleries. They're great places to try *jenever* (ya-*nay*-ver), aka Dutch gin.

What to Drink

Lager beer is the staple, served cool and topped by a two-finger-thick head of froth – supposedly to trap the flavour. Heineken and Amstel are the most common brands. Brouwerij 't IJ and De Prael are delicious local brewers. Besides beer, cafes always serve wine and coffee. The latter is quite popular: the Netherlands consumes more java per capita than any other European country besides Denmark.

☑ Top Tips

▶ Cafe means pub; a coffeeshop is where one gets marijuana.

▶ *Een bier*, *een pils* or *een vaas* is a normal-sized glass of beer; *een kleintje pils* is a small glass.

▶ A *koffie* is black; *koffie verkeerd* (coffee 'wrong') is made with milk, similar to a caffe latte.

Best Brown Cafes

Café 't Smalle The city's most intimate canalside drinking: you can't get closer to the water without jumping in. (p56)

Hoppe An icon of drinking history with a bottomless vat, beloved by journalists, bums and raconteurs. (p152)

Drinking canalside in De Wallen (p31)

Café In 't Aepjen Candles burn all day long at this time-warped cafe in a 500-year-old house. (p34)

De Sluyswacht Swig in the lockkeeper's quarters across the way from Rembrandt's house. (p127)

Best Tasting Houses

Wynand Fockink This 1679 tasting house pours glorious *jenever*. (p34)

In de Olofspoort A crew of regulars has dedicated *jenever* bottles stocked just for them. (p35)

Best Beer

Brouwerij 't IJ Amsterdam's leading microbrewery sits at the foot of a twirling windmill. (p134)

Café Belgique Belgium's best brews flow from the glinting brass taps. (p35)

Café de Spuyt A mellow, beer-rich respite from Leidseplein madness. (p77)

Best Cocktails

Door 74 Ring the doorbell and let the mixologists shake up your tipple. (p78)

Vesper Bar The Jordaan's luxe cocktail bar channels a James Bond vibe. (p58)

Best Outdoor Terraces

Westergasterras A fun local crowd throngs the patio at the atmospheric former gasworks. (p65)

't Blauwe Theehuis A kooky spaceship smack

in the middle of Vondelpark's greenery. (p99)

Best Local Scene

De Twee Zwaantjes Ground zero for traditional drunken Dutch singalongs. (p57)

Kingfisher This locals' local rocks hard come happy hour. (p112)

De Ysbreeker Hot spot overlooking the houseboat-dotted Amstel. (p120)

Best Grand Cafes

De Kroon A windowside perch from which to watch the Rembrandtplein action. (p76)

Café de Jaren Sip on the balcony, watch the Amstel flow by, and the afternoon vanishes. (p36)

CHRISTIAN ASLUND / GETTY IMAGES ©

Best
Shopping

During the Golden Age, Amsterdam was the world's warehouse, stuffed with riches from the far corners of the earth. The capital's cupboards are still stocked with all kinds of exotica (just look at that Red Light gear!), but the real pleasure here is finding some odd, tiny shop selling something you'd find nowhere else.

LONELY PLANET / GETTY IMAGES ©

Specialities & Souvenirs

Dutch fashion is all about cool, practical designs that don't get caught in bike spokes. Dutch-designed homewares bring a creative, stylish touch to every-day objects. Antiques, art and vintage goodies also rank high on the local list. Popular gifts include tulip bulbs, Gouda cheese and bottles of *jenever*. Blue-and-white Delft pottery is a widely available quality souvenir. And, of course, bongs and pot-leaf-logoed T-shirts are in great supply.

Department Stores & Chains

The busiest shopping streets are Kalverstraat by the Dam and Leidsestraat, which leads into Leidseplein. Both are lined with clothing and department stores, such as Dutch retailers Hema and De Bijenkorf. The Old South's PC Hooftstraat queues up Chanel, Diesel, Gucci and other fancy fashion brands along its length.

Boutiques & Antiques

At the top of the Jordaan, Haarlemmerstraat and Haarlemmerdijk are lined with hip boutiques and food shops. To the south, the Negen Straatjes (Nine Streets) offers a satisfying browse among its offbeat, pint-sized shops. Antique and art buffs should head for the Southern Canal Belt's Spiegel Quarter, along Spiegelgracht and Nieuwe Spiegelstraat.

☑ Top Tips

▶ A surprising number of stores do not accept credit cards, so make sure you have cash on hand.

▶ Useful words to know: *kassa* (cashier), *korting* (discount) and *uitverkoop* (clearance sale).

Best Markets

Albert Cuypmarkt Soak up local colour, snap up exotic goods at Amsterdam's largest market. (p104)

Waterlooplein Flea Market Piles of curios, used footwear and cheap bicycle parts for bargain hunters. (p127)

Colourful clogs for sale

Bloemenmarkt Bag beautiful bloomin' bulbs at the canalside flower market. (p68)

Noordermarkt It's morning bliss trawling for organic foods and vintage clothes. (p47)

Best Dutch Design

Frozen Fountain The coolest, cleverest home gadgets and decor you'll ever see. (p61)

Droog The famed collective is known for sly, playful, repurposed and reinvented homewares. (p136)

Hema Design students put their spin on everyday objects at the thrifty Dutch chain store. (p41)

Best Souvenirs

Museum Shop at the Museumplein The one-stop shop for all your Rembrandt, Vermeer and Van Gogh items. (p101)

Heineken City Store The artfully decorated bottles make unique and reasonably priced mementos (drinkable, too). (p81)

Best Sex Gear

Condomerie Het Gulden Vlies Fun setting with a wild array of condoms for sale. (p39)

Absolute Danny Dutch *Playboy* named it the classiest spot for leather, lingerie and dildos. (p40)

Best Books

Boekie Woekie A creaky shop of one-of-a-kind, hand-drawn, artist-made books. (p61)

Oudemanhuis Book Market A moody, old, covered alleyway lined with secondhand booksellers. (p28)

Best Food & Drink

De Kaaskamer Hunky goodness stacks the 'cheese room' to the rafters. (p61)

Het Oud-Hollandsch Snoepwinkeltje All kinds of Dutch candies, including sweet and salty *drop* (Dutch liquorice). (p62)

Best
For Free

While many travellers may bemoan the high cost of Amsterdam's lodging and dining, look on the bright (and cheap) side. Not only is the entire Canal Ring a Unesco World Heritage site (read: free living museum), but every day there is something to do that is fabulous and free.

Best Free Sights

Civic Guard Gallery Stroll through the monumental collection of portraits, from Golden Age to modern. (p28)

Begijnhof Explore the 14th-century hidden courtyard and its clandestine churches. (p28)

Stadsarchief You never know what treasures you'll find in the vaults of the city's archives. (p72)

Albert Cuypmarkt Amsterdam's biggest market bursts with cheeses, bike locks and socks, as do the city's many other bazaars – all free to browse. (p104)

Best Free Entertainment

Concertgebouw Sharpen your elbows to get in for Wednesday's lunchtime concert, often a public rehearsal for the performance later that evening. (p100)

Muziektheater More classical freebies fill the air during lunch, this time on Tuesdays. (p136)

Bimhuis Jazz sessions hot up the revered venue on Tuesday nights. (p146)

Openluchttheater Vondelpark's outdoor theatre puts on concerts and kids' shows throughout summer. (p100)

Badcuyp All-ages jazz shows bring the neighbourhood out to listen on Sunday afternoons. (p105)

Best Free Tours

Sandeman's New Amsterdam Tours Young guides show you the centre's top sights. (p169)

Gassan Diamonds Don't know your princess from

INGOLF POMPE / GETTY IMAGES ©

☑ Top Tip

▸ Free ferries depart behind Centraal Station to NDSM-werf, northern Amsterdam's edgy art community 15 minutes up harbour, and to the EYE Film Institute (see p167), five minutes across the river.

▸ Even if you pay for entertainment at the Concertgebouw, Bimhuis or Muziekgebouw aan 't IJ, your ticket serves as a voucher for a free tram ride to and from the venue, and a free drink in the concert hall lobby.

marquise, river from top cape? Get the shiny lowdown here. (p132)

Best
For Kids

JOE PETERSBURGER / GETTY IMAGES ©

Never mind the sex and drugs – Amsterdam is a children's paradise. The small scale, the quirky buildings, the lack of car traffic and the canals all combine to make it a wondrous place for little ones. And the Dutch seem to always be dreaming up creative ways to entertain youngsters, such as staging children's theatre in a former squat.

Best Top Thrills

NEMO Kid-focused, hands-on science labs inside; a man-made beach with sand and ice-cream stands on the roof. (p143)

Het Scheepvaartmuseum Climb aboard the full-scale, 17th-century replica ship and check out the cannons. (p142)

Tropenmuseum Spend the afternoon learning to yodel, sitting in a yurt or travelling via otherworldly exhibits. (p118)

Vondelpark Space-age slides at the western end, playground in the middle, duck ponds throughout. (p92)

Artis Royal Zoo Extrovert monkeys, big cats, shimmying fish and a planetarium provide the requisite thrills. (p132)

Rijksmuseum Children get their own audio tour to explore the museum's treasures. (p90)

Centrale Bibliotheek Amsterdam Has a whole children's floor with storytimes, reading lounges and books in English. (p143)

Best Kid Cuisine

Pancakes! Even picky eaters will say yes to these giant spongy discs of goodness. (p53)

Het Groot Melkhuis The Vondelpark's fairytale-like cafe sits next to a sandy playground where kids can run free. (p99)

Taart van m'n Tante Fantastically decorated cakes in a whimsical parlour bring whoops of joy. (p109)

Best Junior Entertainment

Openluchttheater Vondelpark's free theatre hosts musicians, acrobats, storytellers and more most Saturday afternoons in summer. (p100)

OCCII The former squat with an affinity for punk bands gets tender with its Kinderpret children's theatre. (p101)

Best
Entertainment

Amsterdam supports a flourishing arts scene, with loads of big concert halls, theatres, cinemas and other performance venues filled on a regular basis. Music geeks will be in their glory, as there's a fervent subculture for just about every genre, especially jazz, classical and avant-garde beats.

INGOLF POMPE / GETTY IMAGES ©

Jazz & Classical Music

Jazz is extremely popular, from far-out, improvisational stylings to more traditional notes. Little jazz cafes abound, and you could easily see a live combo every night of the week. Amsterdam's classical music scene, with top international orchestras, conductors and soloists crowding the agenda, is the envy of many European cities.

Rock & Dance Music

Amsterdam's dance music scene thrives, with DJs catering to all tastes. Many clubs also host live rock bands. Huge touring names often play smallish venues such as the Melkweg and Paradiso; it's a real treat to catch one of your favourites here.

Ticket Shops

You can buy tickets (with a surcharge) via the Uitburo (p80) on the Leidseplein. Comedy, dance, concerts, even club nights are all potentially available. In addition, the Last Minute Ticket Shop (www.lastminuteticketshop.nl) desk in the Uitboro sells half-price seats on the day of performance. Last Minute shops are also in the Centrale Bibliotheek Amsterdam (p143) and VVV (p178) at Centraal Station.

Best Jazz & Blues

Jazz Café Alto Excellent wee club where you're practically onstage with the musicians. (p79)

Badcuyp Boho community space with everything from free Sunday jazz to African dance parties. (p105)

Bimhuis The heart of the Netherlands' jazz scene beats in this mod harbourfront venue. (p146)

Best Rock & Funk

Melkweg Housed in a former dairy, it's Amsterdam's coolest club-gallery-cinema-concert-hall. (p79)

Paradiso One-time church that preaches a gospel of rock. (p79)

The Bimhuis and Muziekgebouw aan 't IJ

OCCII A former squat that gives the night to edgy alternative bands. (p101)

Best Classical & Opera

Muziekgebouw aan 't IJ Stunning high-tech temple of the performing arts. (p146)

Concertgebouw World-renowned concert hall with superb acoustics. (p100)

Conservatorium van Amsterdam Fringey shows and low prices at the city's prestigious music school. (p146)

Best Clubs

Sugar Factory Creative theme nights that hit all the sweet spots. (p80)

Bitterzoet Fresh, exciting dance club that changes its spots nightly. (p37)

Best Comedy & Theatre

Felix Meritis It might be 225 years old, but this arts centre is all about modern, experimental theatre and music. (p59)

Boom Chicago & Chicago Social Club Improv comedy for laughs and getting the pulse of local politics. (p80)

Worth a Trip

The gleaming **EYE Film Institute** (☎589 14 00; www .eyefilm.nl; IJpromenade 1; ☼10am-6pm) opened across the IJ from Centraal Station in 2012. Movies (mostly art-house) from the 37,000-title archive screen in four theatres, sometimes with live music. View-tastic cafes and free exhibits in the basement add to the hep-cat vibe. Take the 'Buiksloterweg' ferry from behind Centraal Station; it's a free, five-minute ride.

Best
Gay & Lesbian

To call Amsterdam a gay capital doesn't express just how welcoming and open the scene is here. After all, this is the city that gave the world *Butt* magazine. It's also the city that claims to have founded the world's first gay and lesbian bar, and hosts one of the world's largest and most flamboyant Pride parades.

TONY BURNS / GETTY IMAGES ©

Party Zones

Five hubs party hardest. Warmoesstraat in the Red Light District (between the Dam and Centraal Station) hosts the infamous, kink-filled leather and fetish bars. Nearby on the upper end of the Zeedijk, bright crowds spill onto laid-back bar terraces. In the Southern Canal Ring, the area around Rembrandtplein (aka the 'Amstel area') has traditional pubs and brown cafes, some with a campy bent. Leidseplein has a smattering of trendy venues along Kerkstraat. And Reguliersdwarsstraat, located one street down from the flower market, draws the beautiful crowd (though financial and legal problems have taken a toll on many venues here recently).

't Mandje Amsterdam's oldest gay bar is a trinket-covered beauty. (p35)

Getto A younger crowd piles in for cheap food and Red Light people-watching. (p36)

Café de Barderij Gay regulars and tourists mingle over canal views and meaty specials. (p35)

Saarein The original sisters' cafe, democratised for one and all. (p58)

Mr B For all your jaw-dropping leather, fetish and dungeon wear. (p41)

☑ Top Tips

▶ Gay Amsterdam (www.gayamsterdam.com) lists hotels, shops, restaurants and clubs, and provides maps.

▶ The Pride Festival (www.weareproud.nl) rages the first week in August.

▶ Located behind the Westerkerk (p50), Pink Point (www.pinkpoint.org) is part information kiosk, part souvenir shop. Get details on GLBT hangouts and social groups.

Best
Tours

AFP / GETTY IMAGES ©

Best Walking Tours

Prostitution Information Centre Red Light District Tour (www.pic-amsterdam.com; Enge Kerksteeg 3; tours €15; ⏰5pm Sat) The nonprofit centre offers fascinating one-hour tours of the Red Light District, where guides explain the nitty-gritty of how the business works and take you into a Red Light room. Proceeds go to the centre.

Randy Roy's Redlight Tours (☎06 4185 3288; www.randyroysredlighttours .com; tours €12.50; ⏰8pm Sun-Thu, 8pm & 10pm Fri & Sat, closed Dec-Feb) In-the-know anecdotes about the city's sex life and celebrity secrets feature on Randy Roy's lively 1½-hour tour. Meet in front of the Victoria Hotel (Damrak 1-5), opposite Centraal Station, rain or shine.

Sandeman's New Amsterdam Tours (www .newamsterdamtours.com; tours free, donations encouraged; ⏰11.15am & 1.15pm) Slick young guides lead an entertaining three-hour jaunt to the sights of the City Centre and Red Light District. Meet at the Nationaal Monument on the Dam, rain or shine.

Drugs Tour (www.drugs tour.nl; tours by donation; ⏰6pm Fri) The 1½-hour itinerary includes smart shops, a 'user room' (the tour doesn't go inside) and a look at fake drugs being sold on the street. Tours depart by the Oude Kerk. Reserve in advance. Private tours also can be arranged (€40 per four people) in multiple languages.

Mee in Mokum (www.gild eamsterdam.nl; Kalverstraat 92; tours €7.50; ⏰11am & 2pm Tue-Sun) These low-priced walkabouts are led by senior-citizen volunteers who often have personal recollections to add. The tours can be a bit hit or miss, depending on the guide, but are well worth the value. They depart from the cafe in the Amsterdam Museum.

Urban Home & Garden Tours (☎688 12 43; www .uhgt.nl; tours incl drink €32; ⏰10.30am Fri, 11.30am Sat, 12.30pm Sun mid-Apr–mid-Oct) These well-regarded tours visit 18th-century, 19th-century and contemporary Amsterdam dwellings.Tours take 2½ to three hours. Reserve ahead – the meeting point for tours (near Rembrandtplein) will be revealed after you do. Call for last-minute bookings (☎06 2168 1918).

Best
Cycling

LONELY PLANET / GETTY IMAGES ©

Bicycles are more common than cars in Amsterdam. Everyone cycles: young, old, clubgoers in high heels, cops on duty, and bankers in suits. Pedalling not only puts you shoulder to shoulder with locals, it puts the whole bloomin' city within easy reach. And it's easy to get rolling, so don't be shy.

Rental shops are everywhere, and renting a bike is easy (see p175). Vondelpark and the Eastern Islands and Docklands are easy destinations for DIY cycling.

Feeling more ambitious? Travel 20 minutes north of the city centre, and the landscape morphs to windmills, cows and wee farming communities – all accessible via an afternoon bicycle ride. Here's how: take your wheels onto the free Buiksloterweg ferry behind Centraal Station, and cross the IJ River. The ride takes about five minutes, and boats depart continuously throughout day. Then pedal north along the Noordhollands Kanaal. Within a few kilometres you're in the countryside. Cycling maps are available at the VVV office (p178) by Centraal Station. Tour companies also cover the area.

Best Cycling Tours

Mike's Bike Tours
(📞 622 79 70; www.mikes biketours.com; Kerkstraat 134; tours €22) Fantastic four-hour tours take you around the centre of town and south along the Amstel river, past dairy farms and windmills. Reserve in advance.

Orangebike (📞 528 99 90; www.orangebike.nl; Singel 233; tours €15-33) Offers several three-hour cycling jaunts, from a traditional see-the-sights Historic City Tour to themed options (Dutch snacks, beer, Eastern Harbour architecture, countryside journeys). Reserve in advance.

Yellow Bike (📞 620 69 40; www.yellowbike.nl; Nieuwezijds Kolk 29; 2hr city tours €19.50, 4hr countryside tours €29.50) Yellow Bike offered the original Amsterdam bike tour, so it's got it down pat. Choose from city tours or the longer countryside tour through the pretty Waterland district to the north. Reservations recommended.

Survival Guide

Survival Guide

Before You Go

When to Go

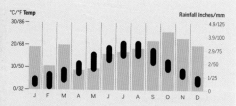

➜ **Winter (Dec–Feb)**
Ice-skating fun, cosy
cafes with fireplaces and
low-season rates ease
the dark, chilly days.

➜ **Spring (Mar–May)** Tulip time! Crowds amass
around Queen's Day (30
April). Alternating rainy
and gorgeous weather.

➜ **Summer (Jun–Aug)**
Peak season, warm with
lots of daylight, cafe
terraces boom, festivals
aplenty.

➜ **Autumn (Sep–Nov)**
Can be rainy, off-peak
rates return, the regular
cultural season starts up.

Book Your Stay

☑ **Top Tip** Book as far
in advance as possible,
especially in summer, and
for weekends anytime of
the year.

➜ Properties often include
the 5.5% city hotel tax in
quoted rates; ask before
booking.

➜ If you're paying by credit
card, some hotels add a
surcharge of up to 5%.

Useful Websites

Lonely Planet (http://
hotels.lonelyplanet.com)
Find reviews and make
bookings.

I Amsterdam (www
.iamsterdam.com) Hotels,
B&Bs and hostels on the
city's official website.

Citymundo (www
.citymundo.com) Reliable
apartment rentals; three-
night minimum.

Hotels.nl (www.hotels
.nl) For deals on larger
properties.

Best Budget

CocoMama (www
.cocomama.nl) Only in
Amsterdam: a red-cur-
tained boutique hostel in
an old brothel.

**Bicycle Hotel Amster-
dam** (www.bicycle
hotel.com) Another
Amsterdam speciality: a
bed-and-bike with eco-
friendly trimmings.

**Stadsdoelen Youth Hos-
tel** (www.stayokay.com)
Bustling, backpacker digs
near Nieuwmarkt square.

Hotel Brouwer (www
.hotelbrouwer.nl) Eight
rooms fill a 17th-century
canal house.

Best Midrange

Collector (www.the
-collector.nl) Offbeat B&B
with backyard chickens in
the Old South.

Backstage Hotel (www
.backstagehotel.com)
Rock-and-roll hotel near
Leidseplein hosts musi-
cians from the cool-cat
clubs nearby.

Hotel Fita (www
.hotelfita.com) Sweet
little family-owned hotel
a stone's throw from the
Museumplein.

**Hotel Residence Le
Coin** (www.lecoin.nl)
Shiny, university-owned
apartments in the historical centre.

Best Top End

Seven One Seven
(www.717hotel.nl) Hyper-
plush, canalside rooms
and luxury service.

Hotel the Exchange
(www.exchangeamster
dam.com) Wild, high-
style rooms designed by
local fashion students.

College Hotel (www
.thecollegehotel.com)
Trendy, celebrity-favour-
ite boutique run by hotel-
school students.

Hotel de L'Europe (www
.leurope.nl) Newly reno-
vated landmark oozing
Victorian elegance.

Arriving in
Amsterdam

☑ **Top Tip** For the best
way to get to your accom-
modation, see p17.

Journey Planner

Journey Planner
(www.9292ov.nl) cal-
culates routes, costs
and travel times,
and will get you
from door to door,
wherever you're
going in the city.

From Schiphol
Airport (AMS)

Train Trains run to
Amsterdam's Centraal
Station (€3.80 one way,
20 minutes) 24 hours
a day. From 6am to
12.30am they go every
10 to 15 minutes; hourly
in the wee hours. To buy
tickets, you need cash
or a credit card with chip
(usually only Dutch ones
work). Ticket machines
accept coins only. To use
euro bills, head past the
machines to the ticket
windows and purchase
tickets from an agent for
a €0.50 surcharge.

Door-to-door van
A shuttle bus is run by
Connexxion (www
.airporthotelshuttle.nl; one
way/return €16/26) from
the airport to several
hotels every 30 minutes
6am to 9pm. Look for

Tickets & Passes

➜ The GVB offers handy, unlimited-ride passes for one/two/three/four/five/six/seven days (€7.50/ 12/16/20.50/25/28.50/31), valid on trams, buses and the metro.

➜ Passes are available at the GVB office, VVV offices (one- to four-day passes only) and from tram conductors (one-day passes only).

➜ The I Amsterdam Card (see p176) also includes a travel pass.

the Connexxion desk by Arrivals 4.

Bus Bus 197 (€4 one way, 25 minutes) is the quickest way to places by the Museumplein or Leidseplein. It departs outside the arrivals hall door.

Taxi Twenty to 30 minutes to the centre (longer in rush hour), €45 to €50. The taxi stand is just outside the arrivals hall door.

From Centraal Station (CS)

Tram Eleven of Amsterdam's 16 tram lines stop at Centraal Station, and then fan out to the rest of the city. For trams 4, 9, 16, 24, 25 and 26, head far to the left (east) when you come out of the station's main entrance; look for

the 'A' sign. For trams 1, 2, 5, 13 and 17, head to the right and look for the 'B' sign.

Taxi Taxis queue near the front entrance. Should be €10 to €15 for destinations in the centre, canal ring or Jordaan.

Getting Around

Tram
☑ **Best for...** Most sightseeing and neighbourhood destinations.

➜ Fast, frequent trams operate between 6am and 12.30am.

➜ Tickets are smartcards called the **OV-chipkaart** (www.ov-chipkaart.nl).

➜ On trams with conductors, enter at the rear; you can buy a disposable OV-chipkaart (€2.70, good for one hour) or day pass (€7.50) when you board. On trams without conductors (line 5, and some on line 24), buy a ticket from the driver.

➜ When you enter and exit, wave your card at the pink machine to 'check in' and 'check out'.

➜ The GVB operates the tram system. You can also pick up tickets, passes and maps at the **GVB Information Office** (www.gvb.nl; Stationsplein 10; ⏰7am-9pm Mon-Fri, 10am-6pm Sat & Sun). It's across the tram tracks from Centraal Station, and attached to the VVV tourist information office.

Metro & Bus
☑ **Best for...** Some Oosterpark, Nieuwmarkt and Harbour spots.

➜ The metro and buses primarily serve outer districts. Fares are the same as trams.

➜ *Nachtbussen* (night buses, 1am to 6am, every hour) run after other transport stops. A ticket costs €4.

Bicycle

☑ **Best for...** Rolling like a local, Eastern Docklands, Vondelpark explorations.

➡ Rental shops are everywhere; most are open from 9am to 6pm (at least).

➡ Prices for single-speed 'coaster-brake' bikes average €12.50 per 24-hour period. Bikes with gears and handbrakes cost more.

➡ You'll have to show a passport or European national ID card, and leave a credit card imprint or pay a deposit (usually €50).

➡ **MacBike** (www .macbike.nl) is the most touristy rental company. Bikes are equipped with big signs that say 'look out!' to locals. But it has handy locations at Centraal Station (Stationsplein 5) and near Leidseplein (Weteringschans 2). It also sells great maps.

➡ **Mike's Bike Tours** (📞622 79 70; www .mikesbiketours.com; Kerkstraat 134) and **Black Bikes** (📞670 85 31; www .black-bikes.com; Nieuwezijds Voorburgwal 146) rent signless cruisers.

➡ Bike locks usually are provided; use them, as theft is rampant.

➡ Helmets are generally not available (the Dutch don't wear them).

Boat

☑ **Best for...** North Amsterdam destinations such as EYE Film Institute, NDSM-werf.

➡ Free ferries to Amsterdam-Noord depart from piers behind Centraal Station.

➡ The ride to Buikslot-erweg is the most direct (five minutes) and runs 24 hours.

➡ Another boat runs to NDSM-werf (15 minutes) between 7am (from 9am weekends) and midnight.

➡ Another goes to IJplein (6.30am to midnight).

➡ Bicycles are permitted on all routes.

Taxi

☑ **Best for...** Late-night travels; if you have lots of luggage.

➡ Find taxis at stands at Centraal Station, Leidseplein and a few hotels, or call one; **Taxicentrale Amsterdam** (TCA; 📞777 77 77; www.tcataxi.nl) is the most reliable.

➡ Fares are meter-based. The meter starts at €2.65, then it's €1.95 per

km thereafter. A ride from Leidseplein to the Dam runs about €12.

➡ A nice alternative when available are the open, three-wheeled scooters of **TukTuk Company** (www.tuktukcompany.nl; 🕐10pm-3am Fri & Sat) and **Bicycle Taxis** (www .fietstaxiamsterdam.nl). They often have lower rates, and can be flagged down in the street, especially near Leidseplein and Rembrandtplein.

Train

☑ **Best for...** Trips beyond the city.

➡ Amsterdam has very convenient train connections with other European capitals.

➡ For national train schedules (including to/from Schiphol Airport), see **NS** (www.ns.nl). For international booking and information, see **NS Hi-speed** (www.nshispeed.nl).

➡ There are ticket sales windows in Centraal Station (on the west side) for both national and international destinations.

➡ Note you'll need cash to buy tickets unless you have a credit card with a chip.

Car & Motorcycle

➡ Parking is expensive and scarce.

➡ Street parking in the centre costs around €5/29 per hour/day.

➡ It's better to use a park-and-ride lot at the edge of town. A nominal fee (around €8 per 24 hours) also gets you free public transport tickets. For more information see www.bereikbaar .amsterdam.nl.

➡ All the big multinational rental companies are in town; many have offices on Overtoom, near the Vondelpark. Rates start at around €35 per day.

Essential Information

Business Hours

Nonstandard hours are listed in reviews; standard business hours are as follows:

Banks 9am to 4pm Monday to Friday, some Saturday morning.

Cafes, pubs & coffee-shops Open noon (exact hours vary); most close 1am Sunday to Thursday, 3am Friday and Saturday.

Clubs Open around 10pm (exact hours vary); close 4am or 5am Friday and Saturday (a few hours earlier on weekdays).

Restaurants Lunch 11am to 2.30pm, dinner 6pm to 10pm.

Shops Large stores: 9am or 10am to 6pm Monday to Saturday, noon to 6pm Sunday. Smaller shops: 11am or noon to 6pm Tuesday to Saturday, from 1pm Sunday and Monday (if open at all). Many shops stay open late (to 9pm) Thursday.

Discount Cards

The **I Amsterdam Card** (www.iamsterdam.com; per 24/48/72hr €40/50/60) provides admission to many museums, canal boat trips, and discounts and freebies at shops, at-tractions and restaurants. It also includes a GVB transit pass. Available at VVV offices and some hotels.

Electricity

220V/50Hz

220V/50Hz

Emergency

Police, fire, ambulance
(☏112)

Money

The Dutch currency is the Euro (€), divided into 100 euro cents.

ATMs

➜ Most accept cards that access the Cirrus and Plus networks. ATMs are not hard to find, but they often have queues or run out of cash on weekends.

Credit Cards

➜ Most hotels accept them, but a fair number of shops and restaurants do not, or accept only European cards with security chips. Some businesses levy a 5% surcharge (or more) on credit cards. Always check first.

➜ For a backup plan against the security chip issue, consider getting a preloaded debit card that has the security chip embedded. Many banks provide such cards.

Money Changers

➜ Try **GWK Travelex** (☎0900 05 66; www.gwk.nl; Centraal Station; ☺8am-10pm Mon-Sat, 9am-10pm Sun; ☒Centraal Station), which also has branches at Leidseplein and Schiphol Airport.

Money-Saving Tips

➜ Make the most of free sights and entertainment (see p164).

➜ Order the *dagschotel* (dish of the day) or *dagmenu* (set menu of three or more courses) at restaurants.

➜ Check the **Last Minute Ticket Shop** (www .lastminuteticketshop.nl) for half-price, same-day seats for all kinds of performances.

Tipping

➜ A small amount is common in restaurants (round up the total to the nearest €1 or €5), taxis (5% to 10%) and for hotel porters (€1 to €2).

Travellers Cheques

➜ These are rarely used – you'll be hard-pressed to find a bank that will change them.

Public Holidays

Banks, schools, offices and most shops close on these days.

Nieuwjaarsdag New Year's Day, 1 January.

Goede Vrijdag Good Friday, March/April.

Eerste & Tweede Paasdag Easter Sunday and Easter Monday, March/April.

Koninginnedag Queen's Day, 30 April.

Bevrijdingsdag Liberation Day, 5 May. This isn't a universal holiday; government workers have the day off but almost everyone else has to work.

Hemelvaartsdag Ascension Day, 9 May 2013, 29 May 2014.

Eerste & Tweede Pinksterdag Whit Sunday (Pentecost) and Whit Monday, 19 and 20 May 2013, 8 and 9 June 2014.

Eerste & Tweede Kerstdag Christmas Day and Boxing Day, 25 and 26 December.

Safe Travel

Amsterdam is generally very safe, but watch your purse or wallet at night in the Red Light District and

Dos & Don'ts

➡ Do give a firm handshake and triple cheek-kiss.

➡ Don't take photos of women in the Red Light windows.

➡ Do dress casually unless it's an overtly formal affair.

➡ Don't smoke dope or drink beer on the streets.

➡ Don't smoke cigarettes inside bars or restaurants.

during the day around the Bloemenmarkt.

Telephone

Mobile Phones

➡ The Netherlands uses GSM 900/1800 phones, compatible with the rest of Europe and Australia but not with North America (though some convertible phones work in both places). iPhones will work fine – but beware of enormous roaming costs, especially for data.

➡ Prepaid mobile phones are available for around €35. You can also buy SIM cards for your own GSM mobile phone that will give you a Dutch telephone number (from €7). Look for Phone House, Orange, T-Mobile and Vodafone shops along Kalverstraat and Leidsestraat.

Phone Codes

Netherlands country code (🖉31)

Amsterdam city code (🖉020) Leave off the first 0 when dialling from abroad.

Free calls (🖉0800)

Mobile numbers (🖉06)

Making International & Domestic Calls

➡ To ring abroad, dial 00 followed by the country code for your target country, the area code (you usually drop the leading 0 if there is one) and the subscriber number.

➡ Do not dial the city code if you are in the area covered by it.

Toilets

➡ Not widespread, apart from the redolent, free-standing public urinals

for men in places such as the Red Light District.

➡ Many people duck into a cafe or department store.

➡ The standard fee for toilet attendants is €0.50.

Tourist Information

➡ **I Amsterdam** (www .iamsterdam.com) is the city's info-packed official website.

➡ The **VVV Main Office** (Map p26, E1; Stationsplein 10; ⏰7am-9pm Mon-Fri, 10am-6pm Sat & Sun), outside Centraal Station, can help with just about anything: it sells the I Amsterdam discount card, theatre and museum tickets, a good city map (€2.50), cycling maps, public transit passes and train tickets to Schiphol Airport. It also books hotel rooms for free. Queues can be long; be sure to take a number when you walk in.

Travellers with Disabilities

➡ Many budget and mid-range hotels have limited accessibility, as they are in old buildings with steep stairs and no lifts.

➡ The city's many cobblestone streets are rough for wheelchairs.

➡ Tram lines 5 and 24 run wheelchair-accessible carriages. All buses are accessible, as are metro stations.

➡ For further information, check the accessibility guide at **Accessible Amsterdam** (www.toegankelijk amsterdam.nl).

Visas

➡ Tourists from nearly 60 countries – including Australia, Canada, Israel, Japan, New Zealand, Singapore, South Korea, the USA and most of Europe – need only a valid passport to visit the Netherlands for up to three months.

➡ EU nationals can enter for three months with just their national identity card.

➡ Nationals of most other countries need a Schengen visa, valid within the EU member states (except the UK and Ireland), plus Norway and Iceland, for 90 days within a six-month period.

➡ The **Netherlands Foreign Affairs Ministry** (www.minbuza.nl/en) lists consulates and embassies around the world that issue visas.

Language

The pronunciation of Dutch is fairly straightforward. If you read our coloured pronunciation guides as if they were English, you'll be understood just fine. Note that **öy** is pronounced as the 'er y' (without the 'r') in 'her year', and **kh** is a throaty sound, similar to the 'ch' in the Scottish *loch*. The stressed syllables are indicated with italics.

Where relevant, both polite and informal options in Dutch are included, indicated with 'pol' and 'inf' respectively.

To enhance your trip with a phrasebook, visit **lonelyplanet.com**. Lonely Planet iPhone phrasebooks are available through the Apple App store.

Basics

Hello.	*Dag./Hallo.*	dakh/ha·*loh*
Goodbye.	*Dag.*	dakh
Yes.	*Ja.*	yaa
No.	*Nee.*	ney

Please.
Alstublieft. (pol) al·stew·*bleeft*
Alsjeblieft. (inf) a·shuh·*bleeft*

Thank you.
Dank u/je. (pol/inf) dangk ew/yuh

Excuse me.
Excuseer mij. eks·kew·*zeyr* mey

How are you?
Hoe gaat het met hoo khaat huht met
u/jou? (pol/inf) ew/yaw

Fine. And you?
Goed. En met khoot en met
u/jou? (pol/inf) ew/yaw

Do you speak English?
Spreekt u Engels? spreykt ew *eng*·uhls

I don't understand.
Ik begrijp ik buh·*khreyp*
het niet. huht neet

Eating & Drinking

I'd like ...
Ik wil graag ... ik wil khraakh ...

a beer	*een bier*	uhn beer
a coffee	*een koffie*	uhn ko·fee
a table for two	*een tafel voor twee*	uhn *taa*·fuhl vohr twey
the menu	*een menu*	uhn me·*new*

I don't eat (meat).
Ik eet geen (vlees). ik eyt kheyn (vleys)

Delicious!
Heerlijk!/Lekker! heyr·luhk/le·kuhr

Cheers!
Proost! prohst

Please bring the bill.
Mag ik de makh ik duh
rekening rey·kuh·ning
alstublieft? al·stew·*bleeft*

Shopping

I'd like to buy ...
Ik wil graag ... ik wil khraakh ...
kopen. koh·puhn

I'm just looking.
Ik kijk alleen maar. ik keyk a·*leyn* maar

How much is it?
Hoeveel kost het? hoo·*veyl* kost huht

That's too expensive.
Dat is te duur.   dat is tuh dewr

Can you lower the price?
Kunt u wat van de   kunt ew wat van duh
prijs afdoen?   preys af·doon

Emergencies

Help!
Help!   help

Call a doctor!
Bel een dokter!   bel uhn *dok*·tuhr

Call the police!
Bel de politie!   bel duh poh·*leet*·see

I'm sick.
Ik ben ziek.   ik ben zeek

I'm lost.
Ik ben verdwaald.   ik ben vuhr·*dwaalt*

Where are the toilets?
Waar zijn de   waar zeyn duh
toiletten?   twa·*le*·tuhn

Time & Numbers

What time is it?
Hoe laat is het?   hoo laat is huht

It's (10) o'clock.
Het is (tien) uur.   huht is (teen) ewr

Half past (10).
Half (elf).   half (elf)
(lit: half eleven)

morning	*'s ochtends*	sokh·tuhns
afternoon	*'s middags*	smi·dakhs
evening	*'s avonds*	saa·vonts

yesterday	*gisteren*	khis·tuh·ruhn
today	*vandaag*	van·*daakh*
tomorrow	*morgen*	mor·khuhn

1	*één*	eyn
2	*twee*	twey
3	*drie*	dree
4	*vier*	veer
5	*vijf*	veyf
6	*zes*	zes
7	*zeven*	zey·vuhn
8	*acht*	akht
9	*negen*	ney·khuhn
10	*tien*	teen

Transport & Directions

Where's the ...?
Waar is ...?   waar is ...

How far is it?
Hoe ver is het?   hoo ver is huht

What's the address?
Wat is het adres?   wat is huht a·*dres*

Can you show me (on the map)?
Kunt u het mij   kunt ew huht mey
tonen (op de   *toh*·nuhn (op duh
kaart)?   kaart)

A ticket to ..., please.
Een kaartje naar   uhn *kaar*·chuh naar
..., graag.   ... khraakh

Please take me to ...
Breng me   breng muh
alstublieft   al·stew·*bleeft*
naar ...   naar ...

Does it stop at ...?
Stopt het in ...?   stopt huht in ...

I'd like to get off at ...
Ik wil graag in ...   ik wil khraak in ...
uitstappen.   öyt·sta·puhn

Can we get there by bike?
Kunnen we er   ku·nuhn wuh uhr
met de fiets heen?   met duh feets heyn

Behind the Scenes

Send Us Your Feedback

We love to hear from travellers – your comments help make our books better. We read every word, and we guarantee that your feedback goes straight to the authors. Visit **lonelyplanet.com/contact** to submit your updates and suggestions.

Note: We may edit, reproduce and incorporate your comments in Lonely Planet products such as guidebooks, websites and digital products, so let us know if you don't want your comments reproduced or your name acknowledged. For a copy of our privacy policy visit lonelyplanet.com/privacy.

Karla's Thanks

Many thanks to Jeremy Gray, Kimberley and crew from Randy Roy's, Roel and Martijn de Haas, and Manon Zondervan for your knowledge and help on the ground. Thanks most to Eric Markowitz, the world's best partner-for-life, who joined me in Amsterdam for steep stairs, beery brown cafes and windmill explorations.

Acknowledgments

Cover photograph: Bridge over Herengracht, Amsterdam; Jean-Pierre Lescourret/Getty Images ©.

This Book

This 3rd edition of Lonely Planet's *Pocket Amsterdam* guidebook was researched and written by Karla Zimmerman. The previous two editions were written by Zora O'Neill. This guidebook was commissioned in Lonely Planet's London office, and produced by the following:

Commissioning Editor Joanna Cooke
Coordinating Editors Andrea Dobbin, Elizabeth Jones **Coordinating Cartographer** Valeska Cañas **Coordinating Layout Designer** Sandra Helou **Managing Editor** Martine Power **Senior Editors** Catherine Naghten, Susan Paterson **Managing Cartographers** Alison Lyall, Adrian Persoglia, Amanda Sierp **Managing Layout Designer** Chris Girdler **Cover Research** Naomi Parker **Internal Image Research** Aude Vauconsant **Language Content** Branislava Vladisavljevic **Thanks to** David Carroll, Melanie Dankel, Stephen Dekker, Barbara Delissen, Ryan Evans, Fayette Fox, Larissa Frost, Suki Gear, Mark Griffiths, Lisa Humphreys, Jouve India, Annelies Mertens, Wayne Murphy, Katie O'Connell, Trent Paton, Raphael Richards, Laura Stansfeld, Gerard Walker, Emily Wolman

Index

See also separate subindexes for:

⊗ **Eating p189**

🍷 **Drinking p189**

✪ **Entertainment p190**

🔒 **Shopping p191**

Eating

Drinking

Our Writer

Karla Zimmerman

During her Amsterdam travels Karla admired art, bicycled crash-free, ate an embarrassing quantity of *frites* and bent over to take her *jenever* like a local. She has been visiting Amsterdam since 1989, decades that have seen her trade space cakes for *stroopwafels*, to a much more pleasant effect. She never tires of the city's bobbing houseboats, cling-clinging bike bells and canal houses tilting at impossible angles.

Based in Chicago, Karla writes travel features for newspapers, books, magazines and websites. She has travelled to more than 55 countries, and worked on several Lonely Planet guidebooks covering the USA, Canada, Caribbean and Europe.

Published by Lonely Planet Publications Pty Ltd
ABN 36 005 607 983
3rd edition – Mar 2013
ISBN 978 1 74220 054 5
© Lonely Planet 2013   Photographs © as indicated 2013
10 9 8 7 6 5 4 3
Printed in China